Jesus: Life or Legend?

Can we know what Jesus was really like? How much of the traditional account is reliable, how much myth?

Nearly twenty centuries have passed since Jesus lived and died. And the story of his life and teaching exerts a powerful hold on the human imagination. Yet over the last few generations many writers have questioned the evidence about Jesus. He has been portrayed as a clown, and obsessive, a new-age guru...

Carsten Thiede looks at the languages, the contemporary sources, the unpublished finds, the Jewish and Roman setting of the time of Jesus. He considers the evidence of the New Testament Gospels, but also the references to Jesus in other writings, including the mysterious 'gnostic gospels'.

Carsten Thiede is an expert in the manuscripts, the archaeology and the history of the first century. He has lectured at the universities of Oxford, London and Geneva. He is a member of council of Germany's Institute for Education and Knowledge. His published work includes The Earliest Gospel Fragment? *and* Simon Peter: from Galilee to Rome. *He lives in Wuppertal, Germany, with his English wife, Franziska, and their young daughter, Miriam.*

*I dedicate this book to my daughter
Miriam, who patiently listened to
the sound of the typewriter in the
months before her birth, while her
mother typed these pages. In the
words of Exodus:*

*'Can any tambourine sound
sweeter?'*

Jesus:
Life or Legend?

Carsten Thiede

A LION PAPERBACK
Oxford · Batavia · Sydney

Text copyright © 1990 Carsten Thiede
This edition copyright © Lion Publishing plc

Published by
Lion Publishing plc
Sandy Lane West, Oxford, England
ISBN 0 7459 1917 0
Lion Publishing Corporation
1705 Hubbard Avenue, Batavia, Illinois 60510, USA
ISBN 0 7459 1917 0
Albatross Books Pty Ltd
PO Box 320, Sutherland, NSW 2232, Australia
ISBN 0 7324 0267 0

British Library Cataloguing in Publication Data
(Applied for)

Library of Congress Cataloging-in-Publication Data
(Applied for)

Printed and bound in Great Britain by Cox & Wyman Ltd,
Reading

Contents

Ancient writers sometimes meant what they said, and occasionally even knew what they were talking about.

George Kennedy

Introduction

This book is something of a detective story. Why, when, how and where did the first Christians begin to write down the story of Jesus, his deeds and his followers? What, or where, are the earliest written sources of the life of Jesus? Who read, who spread the texts? How were they used? Did the existence of the Roman Empire help to turn the 'parochial' beginnings of Christian literature into an international enterprise?

Jerusalem, Capernaum, Galilee, Rome—the destinations of tourists and pilgrims, a magnet for archaeologists and historians—what role did these places play in the first century AD? Is what we know of Jesus all legend, concocted by later forgers and intriguers? Or is there hard evidence to draw on when we talk about the life of Jesus?

This investigation uses the standard tools of archaeology, history, literary criticism, but also draws heavily on more complicated-sounding and some less exciting ones—such as palaeography (the study of ancient writing), papyrology (the study of ancient papyrus manuscripts) and others, to sift the evidence. In other words, the tools I have worked with myself over years of researching and writing.

They have taken me to archaeological sites as far afield as Israel, Greece and Italy, as well as to such manuscript collections as those in the John Rockefeller Museum in Jerusalem or in the Bibliotheca Bodmeriana in Cologny near Geneva, to the archives of the British Library in London or the Vatican Library in Rome. The articles and books so far published as a result have been discussed by other scholars, and this book has actually profited from international debate. Long may that debate continue. Gone are the days when a scholar could 'wander solitary there'.

The book draws on clues old and new, in the knowledge that more may still be awaiting discovery somewhere at one of those many digs all over the old Roman Empire. And it is done in the knowledge that other scholars may prefer different methods of what is sometimes called 'higher criticism' than those applied in this book.

When the 'Sevso' treasure hit the headlines at Sotheby's in February 1990, no one seemed to know the answers to so many questions: where did it originally come from? What is its exact date? Is it authentic anyway? Some circumstantial evidence could be summoned to date it to the late fourth century (which is its style), to trace it to Pannonia in modern Hungary and Yugoslavia (since the region of Lake Balaton is mentioned on one of the plates), and to ascribe it to a Christian, since the Chi-Rho monogram of Christ appears on the very plate dedicated to Sevso. A wealthy fourth-century Christian—and why not? But many questions remain unanswered.

These unanswered questions sum up the predicament and the never-ending challenge faced by all those who are trying to investigate our history. And Christian history has a particular claim to make: after all, it is based on the teachings of the man who said that he was the truth.

PART I

HOW WERE THE DOCUMENTS ABOUT JESUS COMPILED?

In this first part we shall be looking at how the existing written sources relating to Jesus were compiled. For this, we need to step back a little and enter the Roman-dominated, Greek-speaking world of first-century Jews, where speaking, listening and memorizing were educational skills at least as important as reading and writing.

Some of the questions we shall ask are: did Jesus himself leave any written evidence about himself? Were the first disciples ignorant and uneducated countrymen? How did the Gospels of Matthew, Mark, Luke and John come to be written? What about other writings?

1
The Media

Reading, writing, speaking, listening, memorizing—all skills needed for good communication. But was it different in Jesus' day? As we shall see in this chapter, communication was primarily by word-of-mouth—requiring concentration and a good memory.

But first, one question has vexed some of Jesus' followers over the centuries. Did he himself leave us with any written evidence about himself?

A correspondence with King Abgar

There is evidence of a sudden rise in the number of writings about Jesus in the second century. At that time, it is true, a man called Marcion had thought that even four gospels were three too many, and so had edited a 'purified' version of Luke's Gospel as the authoritative one for his followers. But others had felt the opposite urge: things only hinted at in the gospels needed elaboration—the childhood of Jesus, his physical appearance, and, of course, further sayings, actions, miracles. And some of these publications became instant best sellers.

There was good King Abgar 'the Black' of Edessa. Edessa was, and still is, a real place (today it is called Urfa, in Anatolia), and Abgar was a real king, reigning from AD9 to 46. Abgar, it is said, wrote to Jesus, asking him for a miracle healing: 'And when I heard all those things about you, I considered that you are either God himself who has come down from heaven to act like this, or that you are the Son of God doing such things. Therefore I am writing to you and ask you to visit me and cure my illness. Incidentally, I have heard that the Jews are grumbling about you and wish you harm. I have a city, rather small, but noble, and it is sufficient for us both.'

And it is recorded that Jesus replied, by way of a courier, beginning with an allusion to a saying preserved in the Gospel of John: 'Blessed are you, who has believed in me without having seen me.' He declined Abgar's invitation, since he still had to fulfil all that for which he had been sent. However, after his ascension, wrote Jesus, he would send one of his disciples, 'so that he may cure your illness and give life to you and to those who are with you.'

Was Jesus a letter-writer? The church historian Eusebius, writing in the early fourth century, quotes Abgar's texts and tells the story. It has a happy ending, with Thaddaeus going to Abgar and healing him, in the year 340 (that is, AD28/29). It seems that Eusebius did not doubt Jesus' ability to write, and he refers to the archives of Edessa as his source. He does not seem in the least perturbed by the fact that the New Testament nowhere so much as hints at such a correspondence.

Inscriptions on stone, papyri (written documents) and ostraca (pot shards or broken pieces of earthenware) were all used between the third and the eighth century to spread this 'letter' of Jesus, and it was even inscribed on amulets. However, two other 'fathers' of the church, Jerome and Augustine, writing some seventy years after Eusebius, confirm that Jesus had not left anything in writing; and the so-called Decretum Gelasianum, a sixth-century document, declared the correspondence between Abgar and Jesus to be false. It remained a best seller even then.

But did Jesus write? Was he able to compose something, anything, in writing—or was he illiterate, entirely dependent on educated followers? We know that he could read: chapter 4 of Luke's Gospel describes him reading from the scroll of the prophet Isaiah in the synagogue in Nazareth. And there is a reference in John's Gospel, chapter 8, which tells us that Jesus also knew how to write: 'But Jesus bent down and started to write on the ground with his finger.'

This incident occurs in the story of the woman caught in adultery, and when Jesus begins to write on the ground, he does so in response to the probing, challenging questions of the Pharisees. But note that the evangelist does not say that Jesus drew doodles: he actually wrote (with that finger). Needless to say, generations of scholars have tried to guess what he wrote. It might have been from the Old Testament book of Exodus, chapter 23 verse 7: 'Have nothing to do with a false charge', as some have suggested. We simply do not know.

Why, then, did Jesus never write complete texts, set down his teachings, authorize a literary, theological work for posterity, give us first-hand knowledge of his innermost thoughts and ideas? This questions have been puzzling people since the first centuries AD.

Teaching by word-of-mouth

Jesus was a teacher, living in a social environment where instruction was given by the spoken word, and where practically the only common literary material used to support the teacher's instruction was the written Word of God, the thirty-nine books of what we now call the Old Testament.

A good instructor would have phrased his most important teachings in such a way that they could be easily memorized. And even the average pupil in ancient Jewish Palestine would have been trained at elementary school in the basic techniques of memorization. They learned large parts of the Torah (the first five books of the Bible, the Law of Moses), the Prophets and the Psalms by heart, so a wandering teacher like Jesus would have found a perfect setting wherever he went—as long as he managed to speak in sentences which were clearly structured and marked by rhetorical memory aids.

Even a modern English version of, say, the Sermon on the Mount or the Lord's Prayer, reveals an obvious 'pattern' of rhythm, parallel sentence structures, and so on. Jesus' audience, for their part, would have memorized his words, aided by minds schooled for this very purpose.

The spoken word, the immediacy of the word of the teacher—rather than written instruction—was extremely important. So important that even after the death of Judas and the ascension of Jesus, when a new twelfth disciple had to be chosen, the most important criterion was that the candidate had to be someone who had heard Jesus speak, had heard him teach, had—by implication—memorized his words. In the first chapter of the book of Acts, verses 21 and 22, Peter says: 'Therefore it is necessary to choose one of the men who have been with us the whole time the Lord Jesus went in and out among us, beginning from John's baptism to the time when Jesus was taken up from us. For one of these must become a witness with us of his resurrection.'

Speaking, writing, listening

In AD180, a book was published which was meant to be read as a type of early Christian historical novel: the *Acts of Peter*. It tells the story of the apostle Peter in Rome, and is full of good, edifying stuff with high entertainment value: a contest with Simon the Magician; Peter fleeing Rome and being stopped by Jesus (the famous '*Quo Vadis?*' story); Peter, finally, crucified with his head downwards, preaching to his crucifiers.

History? Legend? No historian will ever want to dismiss such stories completely out of hand. Peter *was* in Rome, and Peter was crucified there with his head downwards: these are facts reported by early historians. But, as in any historical novel, there were embellishments.

For example, what can one make of the following story, told in the twentieth chapter of the *Acts of Peter*: the apostle enters the house of one Senator Marcellus, goes into the dining-room and notices that 'the gospel' scroll is being read. He takes the scroll and rolls it up, then proceeds to tell the story himself from memory, and interprets it. It is about the incident on that mountain in Upper Galilee, where Jesus was 'transfigured' before Peter, James and John. Mark's Gospel, chapter 9, tells how 'a cloud enveloped them, and a voice came from the cloud: "This is my Son, whom I love. Listen to him!"'

In the New Testament, it is told both in the Gospels, and in the first chapter of the letter known as 2 Peter. In this scene in the *Acts of Peter*, Peter even refers to both accounts: 'What *we* have written,' he says. The anonymous author of the *Acts of Peter* chose an incident of which Peter could indeed be claimed to be the best eyewitness authority.

This short passage is bristling with implicit statements which are regarded as extremely controversial by many modern scholars: that there was a complete Gospel of Mark while Peter was still alive and on another visit to Rome; that the first Roman Christians still used scrolls, not book-like codices; that Peter was in fact the author of 2 Peter. But this 'Bible study group' scene also tells us something much less controversial, though equally illuminating: as long as an eyewitness was at hand, his *spoken* teaching was considered more important than a *written* Gospel in the same room: Peter takes the scroll and rolls it up.

It is interesting to note also that not every member of that group had their own scroll. There was just one copy of the Gospel and it was being read to them. Whatever form the tradition took in those early days, oral or written, there was another element involved: listening. People were trained to listen, to concentrate and to memorize. So it is not surprising that the authors composed their writings accordingly—not dry accounts but lively stories, compact units of teaching, and in everyday language.

Those who saw Alec McCowan's performance of Mark's Gospel in the theatre or on television a few years ago, or who have attended an evening with Paul Alexander reciting John's Gospel from memory, will know that this immediacy of the style and the language, and the sheer literary fascination, still work today, even in translation.

As tradition has it, the Gospel of Mark, based on Peter's oral teaching, only came into existence after Peter had left Rome, with his flock not knowing if he would be coming back. They were desperate for a lasting source of information which Mark then obligingly provided. Not much later, a master letter-writer, John, the author of three New Testament letters, tells us that he regards writing as a poor, if necessary, substitute for the spoken word: 'I have much to write to you,' he says at the end of his second letter, 'but I do not want to use paper and ink. Instead I hope to visit you and talk with you face to face so that our joy may be complete.' Here also it was geographical distance which demanded a literary form of communication.

Needless to say, they all knew that a story or some teaching *once written down* would be a valuable document. 'I charge you before the Lord to have this letter read to all the brothers,' Paul writes at the very end of the first of his two letters to the Thessalonians. And, again, at the end of his letter to the Colossians we read: 'After this letter has been read to you, see that it is also read in the church of the Laodiceans and that you in turn read the letter from Laodicea.'

The end of the last book of the New Testament, Revelation, has this to say: 'I warn everyone who hears the words of prophecy of this book: If anyone adds to them, God will add to him the plagues described in this book. And if anyone takes words away from this book of prophecy, God will take away from him his share in the tree of life and in the holy city, which are described in this book.'

Were the first disciples illiterate?

Let us pause for a moment and think about the people involved here—the speakers, the writers, and listeners—those early followers of Jesus. Do we take them seriously enough? Are we prepared to grant them a certain level of intelligence and education, and such critical faculties as we like to see in ourselves—or do we look down upon them as a motley group of gullible semi-literates whose every word and action we have to scrutinize from our advanced and 'sophisticated' vantage-point?

An unbiased witness, the Roman philosopher Seneca, has something interesting to say here. Seneca lived from 4BC to AD65 and was therefore an exact contemporary of the first Christians. In his essay *On Superstition*, a work of which only fragments have survived, he contrasts the Jews with his own fellow Romans. 'They, in any case, know the causes of their religious customs; the majority of our people are doing things not knowing why they are doing them.' As Seneca was no friend of the Jews, he pays this compliment grudgingly and therefore all the more plausibly.

The very first Christians, the circle of disciples and apostles, were all Jews. And, initially, the Romans regarded the Christians as a Jewish sect—so much so that even after Nero's persecution of the Christians in AD64/65, pagan Romans sometimes found it difficult to distinguish between the Jews and their Christian 'offspring'. Seneca's judgment is therefore a pertinent piece of information. The people Jesus had gathered around him must have had some education, enough to put them, in this respect at any rate, above the people who ruled the Empire. In fact, as we might interpret Seneca's statement in its context, these Jews (and by implication Jewish Christians) were already fully 'de-mythologized': they knew about the origins of their faith and its ritual forms, whereas the majority of the Romans were still embedded in ignorant superstition.

In the letter known as 2 Peter, we read this about the

transfiguration of Jesus: 'We did not follow cleverly invented stories ['myths' in the Greek] when we told you about the power and coming of our Lord Jesus Christ, but we were eyewitnesses of his majesty.' Exactly what Seneca had implied: here we have people who insist on first-hand knowledge, shunning the mythological fabrication of others.

But again, who were these people, these eyewitnesses, disciples, apostles? Was there anything about them, any hidden or obvious quality, that would have qualified them to 'deserve' their status, and authorized them to write about their experiences with Jesus, should the need to do so arise? Would Jesus have looked for such qualities at all, in view of his intended 'world mission', recorded at the end of Matthew's Gospel? This is a daunting command: 'Go and make disciples of all nations...teaching them to obey everything I have commanded you...' Not an easy task for people who were Galilean backwoodsmen, one might think. Or were they?

2

The Multilingual World of the New Testament

It is one of the myths surrounding the New Testament that the first disciples were poor and simple people and that one of the miraculous hallmarks of Christianity is that its message was spread by and indeed entrusted to such people. Far from it! We do not know much about the biographical background of the twelve apostles, but what we do know about some of them reveals a completely different picture.

Schooling in New Testament times

The ability to read and write was common among male Jews; it was part of their basic education. Learning had to operate in two languages—Aramaic and Hebrew. Aramaic was the 'native tongue', the everyday language, of Jews in first-century Palestine. But the Scriptures, our Old Testament, were not written in Aramaic—with a few exceptions, particularly in the book of Daniel—they were written in Hebrew. What was more, the Hebrew texts were written down without vowels and every Jew at school had to learn to cope with written Hebrew. A shortcut was to learn as many texts as possible by heart, especially those used for lessons in the synagogue. Every adult male Jew was entitled to read the texts and recite the prayers. Rabbis (religious teachers) condemned this custom of reciting from memory: they insisted on the importance of reading aloud from the written text.

Learning long texts by heart was not an easy way out anyway: a good memory and good memorizing techniques had to be developed. And so they had been, not only at school but also in the Jewish home. Flavius Josephus, the Jewish historian who died around AD95—a contemporary of the second Christian generation—tells the story: 'Among our people,' he writes in an attack on a man called Apion, 'you may ask the first person that comes along about the laws [the law of the Torah], and he will recite them to you much easier than he would his own name. Since we learn the laws from the dawning of our awareness onwards, they are, as it were, carved into our souls.' And another Jewish contemporary of the early Christians, Philo of Alexandria, emphasized the training of the memory as an obligatory ingredient of a full education.

In addition to memorizing and reading, writing was another ability acquired both at home and at school. Archaeologists have discovered inscriptions on everyday items—jars, ostraca (shards), even graffiti, some of them with alphabet and calculation exercises. Probably the most famous of them is the Gezer Calendar, a schoolboy's exercise on a piece of limestone. This dates back to the tenth or ninth century BC and demonstrates that writing (and the systematic learning of it) had a long history among Jews well before the time of Jesus.

Then there are the references in the Gospels, referred to in Chapter 1, which record Jesus' ability to read and write. There is also the account in the first chapter of Luke's Gospel of how Zechariah, the temporarily mute father of John the Baptist, wrote down his baby son's name. The astonishment of the onlookers recorded there was not caused by the fact that he was able to write, but by what he wrote.

Even Greek, the international language of philosophy, trade and commerce in those days, could be used in school. Not only in Jerusalem, but also in Galilean villages such as

Tiberias and Sepphoris (about four miles from Nazareth), there is evidence that Greek was the language of the synagogue and also at school—schools were often part of the local synagogue. It may sound amazing, but it is certainly quite possible that Jesus, or his disciples, could have been conversant in three languages from their school-days on: reading, writing, listening and speaking in Aramaic, Hebrew and Greek.

The first disciples

The two pairs of brothers among the first disciples—Peter and Andrew, and James and John—were more than just ordinary fisherfolk, they were fishing entrepreneurs and merchants. The Sea of Galilee was the main supplier of fish for that part of the country and it was also on a main trade route, the Via Maris. For business purposes alone, these fishermen would have had basic skills in reading and writing in more than one language.

Also, John apparently had contacts with the High Priest's palace in Jerusalem. John's Gospel, chapter 18, tells us that he was known to the High Priest and so had immediate access to the courtyard when Jesus was taken to trial. The famous— or rather infamous—labelling of the apostles in Jerusalem as 'unschooled, ordinary men', recorded in Acts, chapter 4, was not based on their illiteracy, but on their lack of any formal rabbinical training. And the reference to Peter's heavy regional Galilean accent mentioned by Matthew and by Luke does not suggest illiteracy. The people in Jerusalem simply had the same prejudice against a Galilean as, say, a speaker of Oxford English today might have against someone with a rural accent.

When Peter took on the role as the first head of the Christian community after Jesus' ascension—a role Jesus himself had entrusted to him, he was totally at ease speaking to thousands of people. Chapters 2 and 3 of the Acts of the Apostles show Peter's facility to interpret and apply the

Scriptures; later he was able to confront the Sanhedrin, the ruling body of religious leaders, using their own rhetorical weapons. He also spent days in the household of a high-ranking Roman army officer, a centurion called Cornelius, explaining—apparently in Greek, for Roman army men would not normally have known Aramaic—the message of Jesus, leading them to belief and baptism.

One might say, of course, that all this was the Holy Spirit's doing (see Acts 4:8), but not even the New Testament claims that this was all there was to it. Peter had not been an empty vessel. When he joined Jesus, he had apparent gifts, raw talents, enormous spontaneity; he was eager to learn, ready to repent (after his betrayal of Jesus, see Luke 22:60–62), and ready to assume responsibility after his reinstatement (see John 21:15–21). This is how the Holy Spirit could work through him: not by the miracle of making a dimwit the brilliant leader of a community, but by guiding and strengthening a man who was educated, who possessed qualifications, who had intelligence.

Another disciple, Levi-Matthew, was despised by 'the Pharisees and the teachers of the Law', Luke's Gospel tells us. A tax-collector, he was held in contempt as an exploiter and potential collaborator with the rulers. In modern terminology, he paid the authorities for the right to levy tolls within a customs district. It was apparently a lucrative occupation: even after Jesus had called him to become a disciple, Matthew showed off his wealth one last time by throwing 'a great banquet' (see Luke 5:29) for a large crowd of former colleagues, subordinates and others. In fact, Josephus, the Jewish historian, ranks a tax-collector called John among the Jewish 'notables', underlining the privileged nature of this position.

Archaeologists have recently made out a case for the reasons behind Matthew's particularly privileged position. His tax office must have been at or near Capernaum (the locality presupposed by the story in Mark, chapter 2). Here there was a jetty bedded in mortar, 700m long and 2m wide—

obviously, this town was a major trade centre for fish from the Sea of Galilee. Roman sources tell us that fishermen always had to pay a tax on their catch, and the tax office may have been installed there for this purpose. As the archaeologist Bargil Pixner suggests, if Jesus had simply walked along the jetty, he could not have missed Matthew's office.

An equally plausible explanation might be based on the fact that Capernaum was, after all, a border town. Goods coming from the Tetrarchy of Philippus or from Damascus in Syria and crossing into Galilee would have travelled along the Via Maris which went through Capernaum. In this case, the customs office may have been closer to where the River Jordan flows into the lake, near the junction where the Via Maris is crossed by a road leading to Chorazin and Tyre. It is of course equally possible that instead of there being two tax offices, they were combined in one at the lakeside on that jetty: those who came from the Tetrarchy or from Damascus would have had to go this way if they wanted to continue into Galilee along the lakeside.

So Levi-Matthew must have had one of the more profitable sources of income in Galilee, living off the taxes paid by others. No wonder that he was regarded by many as a despised social outcast. A man in his position would have been highly literate, and, as we shall see further on, he may well have possessed very special writing skills which would have been useful to record Jesus' teaching.

None of the disciples, not even Matthew, was a member of the ruling classes, of the social or academic elite. But Jesus chose each one of them in the full knowledge of their God-given qualities.

The widespread use of the Greek language

One may wonder why Jesus, a native of Bethlehem, brought up in Nazareth, familiar with Jerusalem, decided to look for his disciples at the Sea of Galilee. The answer is simple. There he could find men at home in real life, not yet 'corrupted' by the luxuries of the city, and yet well-versed in international affairs, fluent in at least one foreign language.

The area between Capernaum and Bethsaida, on or near the Via Maris, the most important trade route from the north to the south-west, was a kind of 'Common Market' crossroads. And people living there—traders themselves, as the fishermen would have been—not only met people from all sorts of areas, but had to converse with them in the lingua franca of the day, common Greek. Someone like Peter, from Bethsaida, a town very heavily influenced by Greek culture, would probably have been as fluent in Greek as in his native tongue, Aramaic. Even his name and that of his brother, Andrew, hint at this: the latter is entirely Greek, and Peter's real name, Simon, is both Jewish and Greek. In fact, it is used in Greek literature as early as the fifth century BC.

Who better to chose, then, for the task of world mission, than men brought up and familiar with several languages, including the international language of the day?

Recent excavations at the fortress of Masada near the Dead Sea have yielded some surprising evidence. It was always known that Masada was not just another fortress, but the last stronghold of the Jewish rebels against the Romans. Masada was their last refuge after the fall of Jerusalem in AD70 and the people besieged there were the most valiant, desperate, nationalistic Jews. Masada finally fell to the Romans in AD73; the mass suicide of the defenders remains a part of Israeli national pride and today some recruits to the IDF, the Israeli Defence Force, take their oaths there.

Among the recent finds at this fortress were fragments of papyri and pot shards with names, sums, notes on the distribution of grain, and so forth: all of them, indiscriminately, in Aramaic or Greek. In other words, even these desperate defenders, who had every reason to despise and reject the international language, which was Greek, accepted and used it as a matter of course. These people were absolutely bilingual. And they were the contemporaries of the disciples and apostles, of the people credited with the first New Testament writings.

In the past, many theologians have cast doubt upon historians' conclusions that even 'ordinary' men in ancient Palestine at the time of Jesus had fluency in more than one language. The existence of Greek Jewish tombstones, synagogue inscriptions and similar scattered evidence confirm the findings at Masada. There, in a people extremely conscious of its bond with God, unusually nationalistic in its political and religious fervour, was an unquestionable fluency in the two languages. If even the nationalistic zealots at Masada, in their last stand against the Roman army, were able to use Greek and Aramaic at random among themselves, there can be little doubt that people like the first disciples, living and working along an international trade route, would have been qualified and prepared to do so.

One last example. Sepphoris had a Greek-speaking school, but it is important for another reason: only four miles from Nazareth, Sepphoris had been the capital of Galilee until about AD18 (that is, during the time of Jesus' childhood and upbringing), and it possessed a magnificent theatre, with seating for some five thousand spectators. The number of people in Sepphoris at that time is calculated at around 25,000. From this evidence the archaeologist and New Testament scholar Benedict Schwank concluded that in first-century Galilee it was not just the upper classes who understood Greek, the language of theatre productions (only a small number of plays were ever performed in Latin outside Italy). Long before the invention of television, the majority of people in this area, from all strata of society, must have known sufficient Greek to enjoy going to the theatre—and they must have done so in great numbers, to judge by the size of the theatre in Sepphoris. Someone like Jesus, brought up in the neighbouring town of Nazareth, would have been influenced by the capital nearby.

Can we actually see him there, taking in what his people, those he was to preach to in later years, were seeing and enjoying? Could followers of Jesus have been theatre-goers, at Sepphoris or elsewhere? Is perhaps the structure of Mark's Gospel, thought by some to reflect the structure of Greek tragedy, modelled on experiences the evangelist had while he was participating in the cultural life of Palestine before he became a Christian writer? Sepphoris certainly is a place to make one think about such questions.

It was a flourishing cultural, multilingual region. And the theatre in Sepphoris was not the only one. Flavius Josephus mentions three further major theatres in existence at the time of Jesus: one in Caesarea, now fully excavated and beautifully reconstructed, another one in Jericho, and a third one in Jerusalem, all built by Herod the Great.

And did the catch-phrases of popular entertainment enter the language? There is an intriguing passage in Acts 26:14; this is in the scene where Paul tells King Herod Agrippa II the story of his journey to faith in Jesus as the Christ. He mentions the experience on the road to Damascus, and what Jesus had said to him there: 'Saul, Saul, why do you persecute me? It is hard for you to kick against the goads.' Here we have, on the lips of Jesus, a saying probably taken from Greek drama. It occurs almost verbatim in Aeschylus' tragedy *Agamemnon* and, in a very similar form, in the same author's earlier *Prometheus Unbound*.

The version in *Prometheus* is particularly interesting, since the words are uttered by Oceanus, one of the Graeco-Roman 'gods'—now supplanted by Jesus, as Paul explained to the Athenians in Acts, chapter 17. Remember that Paul is telling his story not only in front of Herod Agrippa II, who had been immersed in Graeco-Roman culture, but also in front of the Roman procurator of Judea, Porcius Festus. 'Therefore take me as your teacher and do not kick against the goads,' Oceanus says, and in such company an allusion to this evocative scene would have been fully appreciated. The expression had quickly become popular in Greek literature; used by Pindar and Euripides, where it is again a god who speaks, Dionysus. Paul, incidentally, refers to a Greek

26

dramatist on another occasion: 'Do not be misled,' Paul writes to the Corinthians, 'bad company corrupts good character.' This is from a comedy by Menander, but may have had its origins in Euripides' tragedy *Aeolus*, now lost.

Thirteen times in the gospels, Jesus is quoted as using the word 'hypocrite'. 'Hypocrite' means 'actor', and it was Jesus who popularized it in its metaphorical sense. Was it the influence of the theatre which made him do this? Of course, it cannot be proved that any of these sayings is a direct quotation from a theatre play. Since they had soon become almost proverbial, they may have been used as commonly-known sayings; and classical tragedies or comedies were only occasionally performed after the turn of the century—mimes and pantomimes had become the popular form of entertainment.

But think of a preacher today, preparing a sermon on, say, temptation. If he uses that famous quote 'I can resist everything except temptation', by Oscar Wilde, he himself would know (and he would expect a number of his audience to know) the author of the witticism. There is nothing improbable about the authenticity of quotations from Greek drama in our New Testament texts—they fit the evidence, they are an integral part of what we know about first-century Palestine.

The same Jesus who spoke Greek with the Syro-Phoenician woman near Tyre (Mark 7:26), with the Roman centurion at Capernaum (Matthew 8:5–13) and with Pontius Pilate (John 18:33–38; 19:8–11) felt so much at ease in this language that he could actually make a telling pun in Greek. The famous saying, 'Give to Caesar what is Caesar's and to God what is God's', reported by Mark (12:17) and also quoted by Matthew and Luke, plays on the inscription on the coins of Emperor Tiberius current in those days. Between 37BC and AD67, not a single coin was minted in Palestine with a Hebrew or Aramaic letter or word. The inscription was in Greek and everyone was expected to understand it.

Pontius Pilate had coins minted with the word 'Caesar' on

27

both sides. Now Jesus bases his teaching on such a coin with such a word—in Greek, of course, not in Aramaic or Hebrew. This led the scholar Benedict Schwank to observe that Jesus spoke Greek here, in the centre of Jerusalem, expecting his hearers to understand the subtlety of his words. For it is a saying which cannot be translated back into Aramaic satisfactorily, as so many sayings of Jesus can be, not least because the coin on which it is based never existed with an Aramaic inscription.

In this incident, Jesus not only acknowledges state authority in tax matters, by contrast to God's authority which remains above that of the Caesars. He also differentiates quite clearly between the limits of this state authority and the only authority entitled to veneration, namely God's. No matter how many portraits and inscriptions emperors may have had minted on their coins, calling themselves high priests or sons of deified fathers, God was the supreme authority. To argue all this, with a coin, and in Greek, implies a more than average degree of knowledge about the nuances of theology, politics and language on the part of Jesus, and indeed at the end of this incident it is recorded that his adversaries 'were amazed at him'.

Jesus needed followers who could live and act in such a world, and whatever else he many have had in mind when he chose his disciples, the potential for international, multilingual activities, including the knowledge of the single most important 'world language' of the day, were certainly among the qualities he knew he would find.

Even among themselves, Jesus and his followers may have spoken Greek occasionally. Two such instances occur after the resurrection. In John 20:16, Mary of Magdala turns towards Jesus and addresses him in Aramaic, as John explicitly notes, after a previous passage obviously spoken in Greek. And in John 21:15–17, Jesus speaks to Peter using subtle shades of meaning in the Greek words for 'to love', 'to know' and 'flock' which cannot be repeated in Aramaic or Hebrew.

One of the turning-points in Peter's understanding of Jesus took place at a site where these multilingual qualities were taken for granted: Peter's 'confession' at Caesarea Philippi, recorded in Matthew 16:13–20. In those days, Caesarea Philippi possessed two shrines of more than just local importance: a shrine dedicated to the Greek god Pan (hence the old Greek name of the place, Paneas, which reappears in its present day name Banjas), and a temple of Augustus, erected by Herod the Great, whose son Philip named Paneas 'Caesarea Philippi', honouring the emperor (the 'Caesar') and himself (Philip) at one stroke.

So both the cult of a deified Roman emperor and the cult of a Greek god came together at the site where Jesus asked his disciples who he was and received Peter's answer, 'You are the Christ, the Son of the living God.' What a contrast, and what a challenge!

The subtlety of Jesus' choice of this place is even more obvious to someone visiting the shrine of Pan today: the little statuettes of the gods in the empty niches have since disappeared, but one is struck by the huge rock face into which the niches are hewn, with a deep, ominous cave in its middle. Now turn to verse 18 of the account in chapter 18 of Matthew's Gospel, 'And I tell you, you are Peter,' Jesus says, 'and on *this* rock I will build my church, and the *gates of Hades* will not overcome it.'

Jesus expects his disciples to understand the difference between the rock which housed the shrine of Pan and the rock on which he was to build his church. And, in the same statement, he promises to Peter and the other disciples that the world of the pagan religions—symbolized by the cave, the 'gate' of which yawns darkly before them—would not be able to overcome the new church.

With some justification, allusions to Old Testament imagery have been found in the expression 'the gates of Hades' (or 'Sheol', in Hebrew, as in Isaiah 38:10). One does not have to choose between these two interpretations. They are both parts of the many-layered picture of the world Jesus presents to his disciples. The traditional Jewish concept of the 'gates of Sheol'—the gates of death which will not overcome the new, everlasting community founded by Jesus, is there. And the new 'strategic' concept is there— the challenge to take the message to the pagan peoples, with the promise that the underworld of Greek religion and mythology will not prove the stronger. And what better symbol to choose for this than Pan, the god who was often thought to be the 'god of all' in Greek philosophy and mysticism. No—these gods, and their mythological 'gates of death' would not prevail.

This gospel passage is obviously based on an eyewitness account (Matthew himself?), since it depends, as we have seen, on a knowledge of the particular features of the locality at Caesarea Philippi.

3

The accounts of Jesus' life—and how they were written down

It is a surprising scenario: Jesus' first disciples and his first audiences were not, after all, from an uneducated, semi-literate section of society, they were a multilingual group, with mutually complementary abilities and some special skills.

And in those very first days of Jesus' preaching as a wandering teacher, the foundation stones of the literary tradition which later led to the writing of the historical texts may have been laid.

The written tradition—how did it start?

Those who followed Jesus, who went with him, such as the disciples and many others—we read of seventy-two men (Luke 10:1) and of 'many women' (Matthew 27:55)—did not have to take notes. On the one hand, they could rely on their well-trained memories, on the other, Jesus would repeat his most important teachings and so they would hear them more than once.

But what about those who stayed behind, in the villages and in the country? Would they not have wanted to keep 'memos', a brief outline or summary of the main points? Scholars who have been thinking about the customs of audiences in first century Palestine think this is possible. And why not? Writing tablets such as the one Zechariah used in Luke, chapter 1, usually consisting of wax in a wooden frame, were easily available, as were shards of pottery, known as ostraca, handy for brief notes or even lengthy texts (whole letters and literary texts have been found on such ostraca, in fact people could use the same ink on them as on papyri—only rarely would one incise them with a special stylus). So an eyewitness who might have wanted to repeat or pass on one of Jesus' sermons to someone else could have looked at his wax tablet or shard 'summary' and would have been able to reconstruct the teaching thanks to his well-trained memory.

And it is possible to go one step further. Among the writing techniques well-established since the first century BC was shorthand, known as tachygraphy. Tiro, a former slave and freedman of the Roman politician and orator Cicero, who had lived from 106 to 43BC, had refined earlier 'fast writing' techniques and so invented the 'Tironian notes', a method of shorthand which remained in use, with minor modifications, well into the Middle Ages.

There is a fascinating report about the usefulness of shorthand, handed down to us by the Greek author Plutarch. He writes about a session of the Roman senate on 5 December 63BC. Marcius Porcius Cato had made a speech condemning Catiline and his band of conspirators. And, Plutarch tells us, this was the only speech by Cato to survive, since Cicero the consul had arranged for the most gifted stenographers, who recorded every word in special characters, to be present in the senate house. One of the best known masters of the art of stenography was Titus, son of Vespasian, the man who captured and destroyed Jerusalem in AD70. His biographer Suetonius tells us that Titus was so fast that he even competed with his secretaries for fun.

We even find evidence of shorthand techniques in the Old Testament, in Psalm 45. 'My tongue is the pen of a skilful writer,' is how the New International Version translates verse 1, or, better still, in the Revised English Bible, 'My tongue runs swiftly like the pen of an expert scribe.' But turn to the third-century BC Greek text—the Septuagint, the version most commonly used by Jews and interested pagans in the Roman Empire and the version of the Old Testament usually quoted in the New Testament. Here we find the 'skilful writer' is called an 'oxygraphos', or stenographer. The Greek-speaking Jews who translated the Hebrew Psalms into Greek, in the third century BC, must have had the familiar sight of a professional shorthand writer in mind when they used this technical term.

It was near Qumran at the Dead Sea, in the Wadi Murabba'at, that the only extant Greek shorthand manuscript from ancient Palestine was discovered and dated to the mid-second century AD. Although this was written on vellum (animal skin), papyrus and wax tablets would also have been among other materials used for tachygraphy. And not everyone used 'Tironian notes'. As with modern stenography, if a reader does not know the system, he or she will find it very difficult, if not impossible, to decipher the text. The Qumran manuscript has not been 'decoded' yet.

Could this widespread practice of shorthand writing be found among the followers of Jesus? Among those who would have found shorthand techniques extremely useful in their everyday dealings were tax-collectors, customs officials, men like Levi-Matthew. It would have been particularly useful at a place like Capernaum—the border between the Tetrarchy of Philip to the east and the Tetrarchy of Herod Antipas to the west, a border both on the main land route of the Via Maris and along the shoreline of the Sea of Galilee. Here the business of a customs official like Levi-Matthew involved a considerable amount of on-the-spot writing. And in those days before the invention of computerized office equipment, what better to do than to cope with the rush by using stacks of papyrus leaves, wax tablets, ostraca—and an efficient shorthand writing technique?

So, in addition to the local residents who might have taken notes of Jesus' speeches, we have at least one of the first disciples who could have gone one step further—he could

33

have drafted whole speeches and conversations word-for-word, in Aramaic or in Greek, just as the situation required. And this not only *after* his calling to follow Jesus, recorded in Matthew, chapter 9, but also before: the context of his calling clearly presupposes that Matthew had heard Jesus preach previously and that he was therefore prepared when Jesus came to his office.

A first collection of sayings

For many years scholars have assumed that the first generation of Jesus' followers was not particularly interested in written accounts of his life and deeds. Only the second generation, at about the time of the fall of Jerusalem in AD70, when Paul's letters had long been written, and when the sincere desire for a second coming of Jesus during the lifetime of many first-generation Christians had been unfulfilled, would have felt the necessity for historical documents. Historical documents of sorts, since most of what they were to contain was shaped, according to the same scholars, by the various communities and their particular needs, with no immediate, personal access to eyewitness accounts.

Some scholars are prepared to date Mark's Gospel to just before AD68–70 perhaps—others opt for about AD70 or soon after. Matthew and Luke are placed in the dumping ground of all 'shaky' New Testament texts, the 80s. And John—the 90s are more or less commonly accepted. There are a few, though, who date Mark as early as AD40, Luke in the late 50s or early 60s, John before 70, and Matthew—a thought dear to some who consider it the oldest of the Gospels—perhaps as early as the mid-thirties. Such datings have appeared in recent publications by serious scholars—but they remain onlookers on a field where the game is played by different rules.

Even if Mark's gospel can be dated to AD68, the earliest dating that can demand at least a small patch in the debate, that is still some thirty-eight years after the end of Jesus' life—and perceptions and attitudes tend to change in what, in those days, was the period of about one-and-a-half generations. However, there is no need to worry that such a long time between events and first accounts implies an almost automatic decrease in reliability and accuracy. This is plainly not the case.

The *quality* of the source material is always more important than its nearness in time. A writer composing his account at some distance from the events but with a whole collection of sources (sources such as those Luke mentions at the beginning of his Gospel) may be able to draw up a more accurate picture than someone setting pen to paper under the influence of immediate, most shattering events. If it were otherwise, historians today would hardly be able to write sense about the events that took place in the late 1940s or early 1950s. And just think how much emphasis is put today on eyewitness accounts of the Second World War, an event that began to take its course over fifty years ago?

But let us look at whether there was only a second generation interest in written accounts, ruling out the possibility that more immediate steps were taken to record the events by those who witnessed them. Here we are, back to where we were at the end of the previous chapter. Let us go back to the *real* lives of real people in the early first century.

There is Levi-Matthew, the wealthy, well-qualified customs official, multilingual, at ease with people from different countries and different cultures, who suddenly becomes a dedicated, determined follower of Jesus. He hears Jesus speak and decides that these sayings and teachings should be preserved for others. Write them down later, from memory? Yes, of course. One would always remember the words of this man Jesus, and where they were said. But why not take notes at once? Why not take full-length shorthand accounts, and make use of one's old professional skills?

So we see Matthew taking his shorthand notes of the

speeches of Jesus, as verbatim as possible, in the original Aramaic and, occasionally, in Greek. Even the length of the Sermon on the Mount would not have caused any problems for a shorthand writer. Eventually, Matthew would have had a nice collection of sayings of Jesus, for later use, whenever appropriate. He may have mentioned his collection to others, but in the early days of the church, when preaching was considered more important than the distribution of literary documents even when they existed (see the *Acts of Peter* story mentioned above), he would have seen no immediate need to compose a full-length 'gospel'.

The Roman connection

Years later, in Rome. Was it here that Peter, the eyewitness and close companion of Jesus, told Mark all *he* needed to know to write his Gospel? Three early church historians, Papias (writing about AD100–110), Eusebius (about 265–340) and Jerome (about 340–420), supply valuable information, from first-generation eyewitness accounts (Papias) and from massive archive material (Eusebius worked at the magnificent library of Caesarea Maritima, and Jerome was secretary and adviser to Pope Damásus in Rome) that Peter first visited Rome in the second year of the Emperor Claudius who ruled from AD41–54. With him was Mark, sometimes called John Mark, or John, in the New Testament.

There is a subtle hint in the New Testament about Peter's first journey to Rome. In Acts, chapter 12, the writer Luke gives the account of Peter's escape from the prison of Herod Agrippa I, and his last visit to the assembly at the house of Mark's mother in Jerusalem. Taking the dates of Agrippa into account, this must have happened in AD41 or AD42. And then, Luke simply says: 'And he left for another place.' If Papias, Eusebius and Jerome are correct, then the final destination of this journey must have been Rome.

In fact, Luke himself suggests this. The phrase 'another

place' is also found in the book of the Old Testament prophet Ezekiel, in the Greek version of the Old Testament, the Septuagint. There, in chapter 12, verse 3, it says: 'Therefore... pack your belongings for exile... set out and go from where you are to another place.' A few verses further on, the 'other place' is identified: Babylon. At the time when Ezekiel was writing, Babylon was 'the land of the Chaldeans', a magnificent city, full of splendours and decadence, in a powerful country. But much later when Luke wrote, this Babylon had lost all importance, it had become a backwater, and by the time of Trajan's visit in AD114 it was in ruins.

However, another city had taken over the name of Babylon in a figurative sense: Rome. As such, it is used at the end of Peter's first letter, a letter written in Rome: 'She who is in Babylon, chosen together with you, sends you her greetings and so does my son Mark.' And the book of Revelation has several passages where 'Babylon' is used to describe the decadent horrors of contemporary Rome. Perhaps the most acerbic one occurs in Revelation 17:5: 'This title was written on her forehead: "Mystery, Babylon the Great, the mother of prostitutes, and of the abominations of the earth."' What does it mean? The explanation follows in verse 18: 'The woman you saw is the great city that rules over the kings of the earth.' The great city is Rome.

These passages in 1 Peter and Revelation, and comparable ones in later Jewish and Christian texts, had precedents in Roman literature: playwrights such as Terence or Plautus use the proverbial 'Babylonian' luxury and decadence to satirize people and attitudes in plays written in Rome and for Roman audiences. The philosopher Lucretius does the same and a contemporary of Peter and Luke, the satirist Petronius (died about AD65), continues this tradition in his *Satyricon*.

In taking up this usage—and he may well have been in Rome, and have known 1 Peter, when he wrote—Luke achieves two things at a stroke. Having dedicated his two books, the Gospel and Acts, to a high-ranking Roman official, 'His Excellency Theophilus', using this cryptic reference to Rome he now avoids any embarrassment he might have caused Theophilus had he written openly that a man who had escaped from state persecution had gone, impertinently, to the very heart of the Empire. But at the same time, he gave all those who knew the Old Testament in its Greek version (and that included most Jewish readers of it in the Roman Empire) a tool to decipher the statement should they attempt to do so: Ezekiel providing the clue, 'the other place' was Babylon, and Babylon meant Rome.

So Rome it was for Peter. And Mark probably went with him straightaway. That he was with Peter in Rome at some stage at least is clearly stated in 1 Peter 5:13, quoted above. But all other early sources also confirm that he was present when Peter preached the gospel to the Romans. And Peter could have spent at least two, perhaps three, years in the city during this first stay: when Herod Agrippa died in AD44, the man who had put him into prison back in Jerusalem could no longer endanger his safety. Edicts, including those for 'criminal persecution', ceased to be valid with the death or loss of office of the person who had issued them.

Therefore, in AD44 at the earliest, Peter could have left Rome to return to Jerusalem, with or without stopovers. One way or another, he was back in Jerusalem in time for the apostolic council mentioned in Acts 15:1–29, where he opens the meeting with a first address. And this council can be dated to about AD48.

Soon after AD44 therefore, after the 'exodus' of Peter from Rome—a term used by the second-century author Irenaeus in his brief report about the four gospels, and all too often mistranslated as 'death' instead of 'departure'—the Christians would have asked Mark to write down, in a literary form, what Peter had taught him about the life and sayings of Jesus. And Mark obliged. In Greek, of course, the language understood by Jewish and pagan Christians alike. This, at any rate, is what the first historians of the young

38

church established in their accounts, and what we can confirm from our modern historical position.

When did Mark write his Gospel?

A critical reader may be shocked at the harmonious picture I have just drawn. How *can* we possibly trust the New Testament and the early church historians? We can trust them, objectively speaking, as much or as little as any other documents from antiquity. Trust, in this sense, is not a question of faith (in the way Christians would have trusted Jesus more than, say, the fashionable god Mithras). Here it is a question of the reliability of information about events which we cannot repeat by experiment.

It is true, of course, that our first Christian authors are not neutral. They do not even pretend to be neutral: Luke, for instance, says quite unmistakably that he is writing for a specific purpose: 'So that you may know the certainty of things you have been taught'. But what is the basis for Luke's 'bias'? Not invention, but research: 'Therefore, since I myself have carefully investigated everything from the beginning, it seemed good also to me to write an orderly account for you, most excellent Theophilus', he says in the opening words of his Gospel. A personal view of things—yes. A personal interpretation of their meaning and implication—yes. Myth-making and legend-weaving—no.

There is no *a priori* justification for any historian to cast doubt on the sincerity of Luke or on the statement at the end of John's gospel: 'This is the disciple who testifies to these things and who wrote them down. We know that his testimony is true.' On the other hand, such statements do not ask us to suspend thought and enquiry. We are still in the position of those Christians at Berea who 'examined the scriptures every day to see whether it was true' (Acts 17:11).

In a sober assessment of the existing historical sources, we are entitled to take Christian authors at least as seriously as Flavius Josephus. His objective in writing his volumes of history was, among other things, to please the Roman court, while Tacitus, the Roman historian, who wrote his book in praise of his father-in-law, Agricola, Roman governor of Britain in AD77/78, wanted to 'glorify him through admiration, unceasing praise and imitation'. And there is Livy, who wrote his magisterial Roman History because he wanted to 'contribute himself to the glory of the actions of the people who are first on earth'.

What, then, are we to make of apparently conflicting statements among the sources which we have to use in order to build up a coherent picture of events and developments? Declare all of them unreliable? Opt for one and reject the others? Look for ways of harmonization? There is no prescribed method. An example, relevant to Mark's role as author of a Gospel, shows how such sources can appear to conflict and yet be reconciled.

Clement of Alexandria, the theologian, philosopher and historian who lived from about AD150–214, wrote twice about the reception given to Mark's Gospel. Both statements are quoted by the historian Eusebius of Caesarea, and they appear to contradict each other. In one report, having told how the Roman Christians asked Mark to write down Peter's preaching after his departure, he says: 'When the matter [of the gospel] came to Peter's knowledge, he neither expressly hindered it nor actively encouraged it.' But in another report, Clement states—in Eusebius' paraphrasing—that Peter was pleased at the zeal of the Roman Christians and ratified the Gospel for study in the churches.

These seem to be two entirely different statements. But by reconstructing the context of both, one realizes that Clement, quoted by Eusebius in different contexts, describes a *development*. The first stage describes the collection of the material, the composition of a first version of the Gospel. The second stage is the refined version, the finished product, proof-read perhaps by Peter himself. (Interestingly, Clement emphasizes in both accounts that Peter was still alive when it all happened.) We are granted a fascinating glimpse into the workshop of the first Gospel writer. And it is not left to human judgment alone. Clement remarks that it was the Holy Spirit who revealed to Peter what had been achieved (in other words, that now an 'accepted' gospel had been concluded successfully).

But does all this fit what we know of the real life situation of Mark and Peter? As we have seen, Peter could have left Rome in AD44, or soon after. He was back in Jerusalem in about AD48 at the latest. And Mark? He could have started to write his Gospel, accordingly, in AD44 at the earliest. In about AD46, he is back in Jerusalem from where he joins Paul and Barnabas on a journey to Antioch (Acts 12:25) Since our sources are adamant that the Gospel was written before Mark left Rome, sheer mathematical logic leads to the conclusion that it was written between AD44 and AD46.

Even more can be said about this. On that journey to Antioch, Mark is described as 'helper' (New International Version) or 'assistant' (Revised English Bible). Our translations of Acts 13:5 imply that John Mark was the helper or assistant of Barnabas and Paul. But this is not what the Greek text says. It uses the word 'hyperetes', which may indeed mean assistant or helper. But Luke uses it to read thus: 'They had with them John , the "hyperetes"', he says. 'Hyperetes' is an attribute given to Mark himself, in his own right, not in relation to Paul and Barnabas. What then does it mean?

The very beginning of Luke's first book, of his Gospel, may give us a clue. Here, in chapter 1, verse 2, he names his sources and describes those who provided some of the material as 'servants of the word' (New International Version), 'servants of the gospel' (Revised English Bible). The Greek word for 'servants' is the same as the one used in Acts 13:5: 'hyperetai', in the plural. So is Luke trying to tell us, in Acts, that Mark was a 'servant' in the sense used in the introduction to his own Gospel, that is, the author of a historical source for his, Luke's, book on Jesus? Is the reason why he does not call Mark the 'assistant/helper' of Barnabas and Paul, as our translations wrongly suggest, but 'the servant' precisely this—that Luke knew, when he wrote Acts, that Mark had *already* compiled a gospel when he joined Paul and Barnabas on their journey to Antioch?

Let us assume such a reconstruction, and other elements will fall into place, too. There is that strange incident, described in Acts chapter 13, verse 13, when Mark all of a sudden leaves the other two in Perga and returns to Jerusalem. Paul was offended by this attitude and when Barnabas suggests, at the beginning of their second journey, that they should take Mark with them again, Paul refuses 'because he had deserted them in Pamphylia and had not continued with them in the work' (Acts 15:37–38). Barnabas, however, must have known some good reasons for Mark's odd behaviour and defended him. 'They had such a sharp disagreement that they parted company. Barnabas took Mark and sailed for Cyprus.' (Acts 15:39)

What would have been a good reason for Mark's behaviour? Certainly not laziness, insecurity or lack of interest. Perhaps he had left them and returned to Jerusalem because he had heard that Peter had returned there. For Mark, the 'servant', this would have been the long-awaited chance to show his work to the man on whose preaching it was based. And here, at this meeting or soon after, the second stage of the completion of the Gospel may have begun—the drafting of the one which was to meet with Peter's approval, the one ratified by him for copying and distribution, 'for study in the churches'.

In what order did the Gospels appear?

The next steps are easy to visualize: Mark's Gospel soon reaches the other apostles and their circles. Matthew, too, reads it and is excited by the way Mark has created a new literary genre out of the historical eyewitness accounts of his fellow disciple Peter, influenced, as Mark's Gospel was, by his formative experiences as a reader and theatre-goer.

Matthew realizes the potential contained in his own Aramaic and Greek shorthand 'archive'. Perhaps members of his community prompt him to use the material they knew and may even have heard read to them more than once, in services and study groups, and to write his own expanded gospel. And, with Mark's text as his model, Matthew sits down to write his own Gospel, along the same lines as Mark, but modifying and extending here and there—particularly when it comes to the speeches of Jesus and to certain events Peter himself may have omitted—out of modesty perhaps.

There is the story of Peter's only partly successful attempt to walk on the water, told in Matthew 14:28–33, and the story of the fish and the temple tax (Matthew 17:24–27), which do not occur in Mark. For good measure, Matthew even adds tell-tale touches of his specialist financial vocabulary, memories of the old customs official's days, and characteristic of his Gospel alone. The delightful precision with which he describes the incident of the correctly termed 'stater'—the four drachma coin—and the temple tax, in 17:24–27, is one such example. Other stories unique to Matthew and concerned with financial matters are 18:23–35 (the parable of the unmerciful servant), 20:1–16 (the parable of the workers in the vineyard), 27:3–10 (Judas and the thirty silver coins), and 28:11–15 (the bribing of the soldiers at the empty tomb).

Once again, a reconstruction of the events and their chronological order appear to be contradicted by Papias, our earliest church historian. This man, a bishop of Hierapolis in Phrygia (now in modern Turkey), probably wrote most of his works, among them a five-volume *Interpretation of the Sayings of the Lord*, between AD100 and AD110. Nothing of this has survived intact; all we have are scattered fragments, the most important of which are quoted in the *Church History* by Eusebius. And Eusebius informs us that the source used by Papias was 'the elder John'. R. G. Gundry has demonstrated that this 'elder' was none other than the apostle John himself, whom Papias could have met quite easily. But even if he were simply another 'elder', as a first-century witness he would be a man of some importance.

But we return to Papias' statement about the history of the Gospels: a statement which has puzzled readers ever since. Quoted by Eusebius, it is from Papias' lost five-volume work *The Interpretation of the Sayings of the Lord*. Apparently Papias says that Matthew compiled 'the sayings' (of Jesus) in Hebrew dialect, and that *everyone* (my italics) translated or interpreted them as he was able. If this is a correct translation, it would imply that Matthew wrote first, not Mark, and that he wrote in Hebrew (or Aramaic), not in Greek.

Once again, it is the old problem of words and their exact meaning. Greek is a language that can seem extremely simple. But its surface simplicity is treacherous. The sheer grandeur of Greek drama, poetry and prose writing is founded on a wide range of syntax and grammar, on many different levels of style, and the flexibility of a voluminous vocabulary. Even apparently straightforward sentences may depend on shades of meaning that were obvious to anyone who read them at the time but have become obscure or ambiguous to us. This is something English speakers encounter also: for example, when the Book of Common Prayer speaks of 'the quick and the dead', we find the meaning of 'quick' has completely changed in three hundred years. Similarly, sometimes special terminology is used which depends on the context. How, for example, would an unsuspecting reader of mid-first-century Rome have understood the first verse of Mark's Gospel: 'The beginnings of the gospel about Jesus Christ'? 'Iesous Christos' it says in the Greek text. 'Jesus Ointment' perhaps? Or 'Jesus the Whitewashed'? How could an ordinary contemporary reader, knowing practical, down-to-earth Greek, suspect that *here* 'Christos' is the Greek rendering of 'Messiah', God's Anointed? He will understand eventually, of course, from the context of the whole story. But he will not if he has only a snippet of information.

So, tuned to the nuances of meaning, we may want to delve beneath the surface of the words quoted by Eusebius, from Papias. And a different picture indeed emerges.

First of all, the statement about Matthew's compilation of the sayings of Jesus follows one made about Mark, in which he implies that Mark wrote first. Papias begins by recounting the 'elder' John's opinion of Mark's Gospel. He says that Mark wrote accurately, but not in chronological order, the things which Peter had remembered about Jesus. For, Papias goes on, Mark himself had neither heard Jesus nor been one of his followers, but a follower of Peter's. And Peter had adapted his teachings to the needs of his audience—'after the manner of the maxims [of Jesus]',—not with an eye to compiling Jesus' words in a correctly ordered composition. Thus, Papias continues, Mark had not made a mistake when he wrote some of these things down just as Peter recalled (and structured) them. For he (Mark) had one intention only: not to omit anything of what he had heard, nor to falsify anything in the tradition he had received.

If we then look back at Papias' statement about Matthew, the reference to 'everyone' who translated/interpreted them as best he could cannot have included Mark. And it does not, as we shall see. Part of the solution is in a little Greek word, usually translated as 'for', but much better rendered as 'therefore'—the innocuous Greek word 'oun'.

'*Therefore*' (not merely 'so then') Matthew 'arranged' ('composed') the sayings in Hebrew dialect. He arranged or composed them—in other words he put a new order into something he had received in a form he knew he could improve on. But why 'in Hebrew dialect'? Does this mean that he wrote the Gospel in Hebrew or Aramaic, as even some of the fathers of the church seem to have believed?

The word translated here as 'dialect' (Greek 'dialektos') most probably, however, means 'form of expression', not 'language' or 'dialect' in our modern sense of the word. Papias, referring back to the elder John, is saying that

Matthew wrote using a Hebrew/Aramaic style—a Hebrew/Aramaic way of thinking and expressing himself.

How many failed attempts to find the 'original' Hebrew/Aramaic gospel 'behind' the extant Greek text could have been spared if this simple observation had been safely established before J. Kürzinger finally did so in 1960! And how convincingly other observations fall into place once the 'Hebrew dialect' is understood correctly.

Of course, Matthew not only improves the historical and chronological order of Mark, he also changes the overall approach. His context takes in Jewish traditions of interpretation; he stresses genealogy back to Abraham; he uses the Old Testament from the very beginning of his Gospel to document its fulfilment in Jesus; and there is, as R. T. France once put it, a distinctively 'Semitic' touch to some of Matthew's Greek, such as a Jewish reader would appreciate.

This interpretation is supported in the next part of Papias' sentence about Matthew: 'and everyone translated [interpreted] them [the words] as best he could'. The word tentatively rendered as translated/interpreted is the same which Papias used, as a noun, to describe Mark—'hermeneutes'. The nearest verbal equivalent in English, 'hermeneutist', is not much help. It really cannot mean 'translator', as is often maintained, since the one thing Peter, multilingual as he was himself, did not need was someone to translate something he had said. Literally, it could mean 'interpreter'—but was Peter so helpless that he was unable to express himself clearly?

The word 'hermeneutes' here has the simpler meaning it often has in everyday Greek: a person who transmits something he has heard to others, giving it an explanatory shape showing its meaning. Mark was the one who represented Peter's oral teaching in writing, giving it form which included (but did not consist of) interpretation. To understand it like this does full justice to the word used by Papias. And in his statement about Matthew, all he therefore wants to say is that everyone who received and read this Gospel—'each reader'—would in turn represent this teaching to others as best he could: a reconstruction true to what we know about the way the first Christians dealt with the texts they read. They were read out aloud, 'represented' to the audience who listened attentively.

The nuance in the Greek word, that overtone of 'explaining', or 'exposition', must not be overlooked, though: Papias and John the elder do not mean that Mark merely copied down Peter's teachings as though he had dictated them—although this is how the scene of the composition of the Gospel is often depicted in medieval art. No, Mark was an author in his own right, he drew up the Gospel with personal touches of style, vocabulary and structure, he even 'interpreted'. Look, for example, at the way he expresses the element of fear, of awe in the presence of the holy. Then look at his magnificent ending.

'They were terrified and asked each other: "Who is this? Even the wind and the waves obey him."'

'When they came to Jesus, they saw the man who had been possessed by the legion of demons, sitting there, dressed and in his right mind; and they were afraid.'

'Then the woman, knowing what had happened to her, came and fell at his feet and, trembling with fear, told him the whole truth.'

'But when they saw him walking on the lake, they thought he was a ghost. They cried out, because they all saw him and were terrified.'

'He did not know what to say, they were so frightened.'

'But they did not understand what he meant and were afraid to ask him about it.'

'They were on their way up to Jerusalem, with Jesus

leading the way, and the disciples were astonished, while those who followed were afraid.'

'The chief priests and the teachers of the law heard this and began looking for a way to kill him, for they feared him, because the whole crowd was amazed at his teaching.'

And then what is generally accepted to be the last verse of the whole Gospel:

'Trembling and bewildered the women went out and fled from the tomb. They said nothing to anyone, because they were afraid.'

What a brilliant stroke of the pen—to end on this note of holy fear, of the fear before the God who acts in history. (These verses can be found in Mark 4:41; 5:15; 5:33; 6:49–50; 9:6; 9:32; 10:32; 11:18 and 16:8.)

One difficult word remains in Papias' account: he speaks of the 'sayings' (Greek 'logia'). It cannot simply mean a collection of sayings of Jesus, since this could not accurately describe the second stage of development after the fully composed Gospel of Mark (a text with sayings *and* stories) which Papias clearly saw in Matthew. 'Logia' here is just one of many summary descriptions used for the kind of text we now term a 'Gospel'. The Greek equivalent of this term, 'evangelion', is used for the first time by the writer Justin Martyr, in the middle of the second century, some fifty to sixty years after Papias, and even longer after his source, the elder John. The description of Matthew's book as 'sayings' can be understood by looking at the ancient art of rhetoric. The 'pars pro toto' technique—the part for the whole—in this case refers to the most important ingredient of the book—the sayings of Jesus.

The tendency to put the stress on one part of the whole was carried to extremes in one instance by Clement of Alexandria. In a statement paraphrased by Eusebius, Clement values the importance of genealogies (tracing the family tree of Jesus back to the very beginning of Jewish history) so highly that he infers that the Gospels which contained them (Matthew and Luke) were written 'beforehand'. Whatever Clement really wanted to say, timing is not what he can have meant. Is he merely giving the impression that he was picking out the genealogies and saying that they (and not the complete Gospels) had been written first, before the whole life story of Jesus was reconstructed?

But is a neat chronological system of 'one Gospel after another' really necessary? Were they all waiting for one another, no one daring to begin to write until finally someone—and let us say it was Mark—had his hand forced by an impatient community? Is not another possibility at least as thinkable? There was Matthew, with his shorthand notes; there was Mark taking notes of Peter's preaching; Luke investigating all the material he could lay his hands on, and John very much doing his own thing. Then that first draft of Mark's Gospel mentioned above circulated among the small circle of apostles and their companions. Matthew obtained it, Luke obtained it, and they made use of it for their own purposes, while Mark was busy polishing up his own account. Then, suddenly, Matthew's was 'on the market', and Luke's; and Mark's product, the first to whet everyone's appetite, was last of the three when it finally appeared in its finished form. A fate not unknown to authors and publishers today...

And, within the context of such a scenario, Clement's surprising statement could make sense after all. Whatever the final outcome will—if ever—be, we should not see the Gospel writers as people who waited for someone to make the first move, only to hum the tune of 'anything you can do I can do better' when it happened.

Luke and John

Suppose, then, that the beginnings of the Gospel tradition were sparked off by these two men, Mark and Matthew. One,

49

Matthew, a man from Galilee, a disciple and eyewitness; the other, Mark, a man from Jerusalem, a companion of Paul and Barnabas and a trusted friend of Peter's. Both had made the most of their upbringing, their experiences and their abilities. And eventually their writings were published—they were, as Clement of Alexandria had put it in the case of Mark's Gospel, 'ratified for study in the churches'.

We find such 'editorial comments' in several places in the literature of the early church. Two of them are even contained in Gospels: one in John's, the other in Luke's. John's is the one Gospel that actually claims to *be* an eyewitness account—'The man who saw it has given testimony, and his testimony is true' (John 19:35). This claim is confirmed by the 'editor's' postscript in chapter 21, verse 24: 'This (that is, the disciple "whom Jesus loved", mentioned before) is the disciple who testifies to these things and who wrote them down. We know that his testimony is true.' And then, in the last verse of the whole Gospel: 'Jesus did many other things as well. If every one of them were written down, I suppose that even the whole world would not have room for the books that would be written.'

Whoever added these two verses to the Gospel—and some scholars maintain that the evangelist himself wrote the last one, at a later stage—they are editorial comments. A group ('we') confirms that the preceding account is true, and an individual ('I') states that the Gospel, truthful and based on an eyewitness account as it is, is of necessity only a selection of sayings and events, for a complete report would surpass the storage space of the world's libraries (an expectation now as good as fulfilled by theological literature on this Gospel). And there is a beautiful personal note: 'I suppose' the editor says—a humble note of self-irony, quite characteristic of a Gospel which contains such entertaining items as the athletic sprint of Peter and John to the empty tomb, where the critic feels the breath of the eyewitness on his sceptic's neck.

Luke's editorial comment, on the other hand, can be found only by looking behind the title and the name of the man to whom his Gospel (and its sequel, the book of Acts) are dedicated: Theophilus, called, in Luke 1:3, 'Your excellency' (New English Bible). Two things follow from this dedication: first, Theophilus was apparently a high-ranking Roman official. In the New Testament, the title 'your excellency', or 'kratiste' in Greek, occurs three more times, in Acts 23:26 and 24:2, where the procurator Felix is meant, and in Acts 26:25, where it is given to his successor Festus. So we can assume Theophilus had a comparatively high executive position. And the second consequence of the dedication: it was customary for a dedicatee in the Roman Empire to publish the book. In other words to have it copied and distributed at his expense. Here we have a trace of early Christian editorial politics.

Luke knows a Roman official who has had some Christian training ('the things you have been taught', Luke 1:4) but who needs a solid, well-researched account, 'carefully investigated', and 'orderly'. Luke probably knows the custom of dedicatees publishing 'their' books, so he asks Theophilus if he would agree to have the account dedicated to him. Theophilus consents. As a fledgling Christian, he would have noticed that the community he had joined was not exactly affluent, and so he may even have seen it as his task to help by financing the publication of Luke's book (and later its sequel).

Such magnanimity was not without its perils. Even as a Christian, Theophilus remained 'your excellency', a Roman official of some standing and with responsibilities. Luke cannot put him at risk. Carefully he avoids incriminating statements about people who were still alive at the time which might have put Theophilus in an embarrassing position, leaving him not knowing whether to act, or to keep quiet and be accused of shielding criminals.

The most obvious case in point concerns Peter. Luke relates a first-hand report of the arrest of Jesus, he tells us with peculiar attention to detail that someone cut off the *right* ear of the high priest's servant (Luke 22:50). But he does not reveal *who* it was who committed this act of resistance against state authority (which was represented here by the servant). It has been noted that Mark and Matthew do not mention the attacker's name either. But their accounts of the incident are comparatively brief anyway, and, in the case of Mark, his informant Peter may even have been grateful for the omission of an incident which was much less salutary in its final consequences than the sequence of betrayal, repentance and reinstatement by Jesus.

Luke's case is quite different, however: not only is his account more detailed—he knows that it was the right ear which had been cut off and he knows that Jesus healed the ear afterwards; he also betrays, by his use of language, that he, like Mark, knows the name of the attacker. Both Mark (14:47) and Luke (22:50) use a Greek construction which means 'a certain one' in the sense of 'one we know but do not want to identify'.

The second striking example in Luke's writings is contained in Acts, and was fully discussed above: Peter's leaving Jerusalem and going to 'another place'. Here, Luke himself gives us the clue with which to identify the place. In the incident of the cut-off right ear, he merely intimates that he knows, and we have to turn to John's Gospel (18:10) to find out that the man was none other than the same Peter, the apostle who still was, at the time of Luke and Theophilus, the 'rock' of the church, probably busy spreading the message about Jesus in the very heart of the Empire, Rome.

It was one thing to write about the crucified and risen Christ, who, after the ascension, was no longer an *actual* threat to the authority of the Roman administration, but it was quite another to list one 'criminal act' after another committed by the man who was the leader of the church of which Theophilus had just become a young and still maturing member. However, it should be remembered that Luke was writing at a time when the Roman Empire at large had not yet begun to persecute the Christians. It was possible to mix with 'official' people, and those in the army.

Nevertheless, a dedicatee had to be able to stand and face the possible political implications of a work he published. Luke protects him, and he does so in a sensitive and gracious way.

Luke thus represents a third stage in the development of Christian publishing. After Mark's first shot, on the instigation of the Roman community and with Peter's eventual full support, Matthew compiles a work on the basis of two sources, Mark and his own shorthand notes. Both have to find support for the publication of their writings from within their own communities. And John's situation will have been quite similar. Along comes Luke, the companion of Paul (see Colossians 4:14; Philemon, verse 24; and the 'we' accounts in Acts for evidence of their closeness), and finds a high-ranking Roman who has the books copied and distributed at his own expense.

This mould-breaking approach of Luke's, emulated frequently by second- and third-century Christian authors, may have led to the unlikely claim that the original manuscript of the Gospel (after all, it would have enjoyed quasi-official protection thanks to Theophilus) still existed in Florence in the sixteenth century. The Spanish theologian Jacobus Lopis Stunica writes about a journey to Rome and Florence, where he arrived on 9 February 1521. In Florence, or so he reports, he was shown a Greek manuscript of Luke's Gospel, and those who showed it to him 'believed that it was the autograph of this evangelist'.

PART II

HOW ANCIENT AND RELIABLE ARE THE DOCUMENTS ABOUT JESUS?

I n Part II we shall be looking at what can be one of the most exciting, rewarding, and sometimes frustrating, areas of research—the study of ancient manuscripts.

We shall ask the question: who did write the Gospels? And we shall see how the early Christians contributed to an early revolution in book production.

And we shall examine one of the most exciting, and controversial, finds of this century. The discovery of the Dead Sea Scrolls at Qumran in 1947 gave scholars a completely new angle on the study of ancient manuscripts. And it is here that the contents of cave Seven—as yet only partially studied—have yielded what could be the most significant finds in relation to dating the Gospels and New Testament writings.

4
From Scrolls to Books

We have taken for granted what every reader of the New Testament sees and tacitly accepts when he or she opens a Bible: that the Gospels, those carefully selected and purposefully constructed accounts of the life, words and deeds of Jesus, were written and made public by individuals, not by anonymous communities. But how *do* we know who these people were? Who first attached the names of Matthew, Mark, Luke and John to the Gospels?

Identifying authors

In the hunt for an answer, we can pick up the trail by looking at a fascinating little text written in AD180. It is a record of the *Martyrs of Scilli*, written immediately after the event it describes. Scilli was a town in the Roman province of Africa Proconsularis, in the east of modern Algeria. On 17 July AD180, the proconsul Saturninus (the first Roman official to persecute Christians in Africa) had six Christians, three men and three women, brought before him at his council-chamber in Carthage. The 'trial' and sentencing of these people has been preserved in an accurate word-for-word report. And one exchange contains the clue: 'What are the things in your *capsa*?' Saturninus asks, and Speratus, one of the Christian men, replies: 'The books, and the letters of the just man Paul.'

The vaguely termed 'books' may have been the book-type writings of the New Testament: the four Gospels and Acts, five scrolls in all. But in another manuscript of this report they are identified as 'the venerable books of the divine Law'—that is, the five scrolls of the Torah. This implies a close connection between the Old Testament and New Testament writings, stored, as they were, together in the same container. In fact, wall paintings in the Domitilla Catacombs in Rome show Peter and Paul, each with such a container at their feet, each one containing five scrolls. Here we can assume that the Christians wanted to demonstrate the equal value of these two collections: the five scrolls of the historical books of the New Testament—the four Gospels and Acts—are on a par with the five scrolls of the Torah, the Mosaic books of the Law.

But what really interests us here is the term used for this type of container, which I left untranslated: 'capsa'. This is a technical term used to describe the cylindrical case in which scrolls were stored, both for ease of reference and for transporting. The scrolls were placed in the cylinder on end, and it would have been quite awkward to take them out and unroll them in order to find out the identity of each one. Suppose Saturninus had asked Speratus to identify each of the writings in the 'capsa' individually, would Speratus have answered: 'Hang on a moment, let me just take them all out and unroll them for you.'? Certainly not, for they had, in those days, a useful aid for this very purpose: a small parchment strip attached to the visible handle of the scroll, called a 'sillybos' in Greek. And on this strip was written the necessary information—the title of the work, and, if there was more than one work of the same title, the name of the author(s) as well.

It was a simple and effective method. In a bookshop (they did exist even then!) the scrolls, which were stored away horizontally, with one end pointing towards the customer, could thus be easily identified. The scrolls did not have to be taken from the shelf: all one had to do was look at the parchment label—rather like reading the spine of a book today.

Imagine a scene, slightly exaggerated perhaps, in one of the Christian quarters of Rome or Alexandria. A customer enters a bookshop. 'Could I have a copy of "the Gospel", please?' he asks, and the bookseller hands him the scroll. There was only one Gospel, and all he had to do was to look for a scroll with the parchment strip saying 'Gospel', or, in Greek, 'Evangelion'—the word introduced by Mark to describe the contents of his book.

Years later, our customer returns to ask for a copy of 'that new book, the new Gospel'. He may have asked like this, not quite knowing what to ask for, just like a modern-day customer. But it is unlikely: someone interested in a copy of a new addition to the 'gospel'-literature would have known how to ask in more precise terms. The bookseller, in any case, would have known how to find this particular book. 'Gospel' on the parchment strip would no longer have been sufficient, for now there were two different ones. Now some information about the authors was called for, was necessary for practical reasons. 'Gospel ... after Matthew'. Precisely! And, later, '... after Luke' and '... after John', and, of course, '... after Mark'. Why 'after', or, as most translations have it, 'according to'? Because the *type* of book was known: it was a 'gospel', an 'evangelion', that is: the good news. 'The good news' ... 'as told by' ('after', 'according to', or, in the Greek, 'kata') Mark, Matthew, and so on.

In other words, practical considerations made it necessary to know the names of the authors at least by the time a second work of the same type had been made public. But this information was probably already being provided: that parchment strip, the 'sillybos', usually contained the title of the work *and* the author's name anyway, no matter how many books of the same genre existed.

All scholars, even those who prefer late dates for the first three Gospels, would agree that the four Gospels were written by the year AD100, and that at least the first two were finished by the eighties of the first century. It is frankly beyond belief (and reason) that at such an early stage communities could have invented the names of authors. There were a lot of 'witnesses' who were still alive. In fact, as we saw in the previous chapter, a man like Papias, writing as late (comparatively speaking) as about AD110, still used first-hand evidence coming directly from the elder John. And if we assume, with John A. T. Robinson and others, that the four Gospels were 'on the market' before AD70, the attribution of the Gospels to people who did not in fact write them looks even more incredible, if not downright ridiculous.

Our little scene was exaggerated in one respect: it is not likely that copies of the first Gospel were actually sold openly in bookshops at this early stage. They would have circulated, like the first copies of the other Gospels, in a lively 'exchange circuit' among the churches. Traces of such exchanges can be found in many documents of early Christianity, going back to Paul's letter to the Colossians (4:16): 'After this letter has been read to you, see that it is also read in the church of the Laodiceans and that you in turn read the letter from Laodicea.' But even then, and without bookshops, the fast-growing collections—one might call them archives—of the local churches would have called for the precise description of the contents of a scroll on the 'sillybos' outside.

Someone who opened a book—that is, unrolled a scroll—perhaps to read from it in a service, would have had to identify it for the others. It would not have done to say, 'Listen to this new anonymous Gospel I have got here. Is it actually the second or the third? Well, never mind.' Again, the custom of reading the latest Christian writings at public gatherings is documented within the New Testament. In Paul's first letter to the Thessalonians (5:27) he writes: 'I charge you before the Lord to have this letter read to all the brothers.' This was as early as AD50, the most probable date of this letter.

And Jesus himself is a part of a scene in which the name of the author of a scroll text is given. In Luke's Gospel, chapter 4, we read: 'And he stood up to read. The scroll of the prophet Isaiah was handed to him. Unrolling it, he found the place where it is written...' There follows a quotation from Isaiah chapter 61, with which everyone present would have been familiar—as would many, if not most, of the readers of the Gospel, probably well-versed in the Greek Old Testament. But Luke says, even so, that it was 'the scroll of the prophet Isaiah', not 'a prophet's scroll', or simply 'a scroll'. We can see here that the name of the author was given and used even if it was, strictly speaking, surplus to requirements.

One may still wonder why the names of the authors are not mentioned anywhere *in* the Gospels. In fact, they were practically never mentioned in books in antiquity, nor are they today, of course. The place for the author's name is on the title page, and on the jacket, including the spine. With scrolls, it was the parchment strip outside. And, in fact, at least two of the Gospels indicate that the author's name *must* have been mentioned there, no matter what we know about customary procedures. First Luke, who dedicates his books to Theophilus: one simply cannot dedicate a book to someone without mentioning one's own name somewhere. And John, where it says, in chapter 21, verse 4: 'This is the disciple who testifies to these things and who wrote them down.' This presupposes that the name we now find in our Bibles, 'John', was mentioned somewhere—the place being, as we know, the 'sillybos'.

Such a reconstruction of the basis for identifying the authors' names in early Christian writings takes us right back to the first century. Other sources follow suit: Papias, as we have seen and discussed above, mentions Mark and Matthew by name in around AD110. Marcion, a heretic accepting only a version of Luke edited by himself, mentions Luke by name around AD140, and implies his knowledge of the others (his writings have only survived in quotation); Irenaeus mentions all four Gospel authors by name in about AD180, and so do his Anti-Marcionite *Gospel Prologues* of approximately the same time. From then on, sources which have survived to our day increase in number.

But even earlier than some of these witnesses are several of the extant papyrus manuscripts of the Gospels. And some of them still contain the part where the author's name is mentioned: papyrus p66, of the Gospel of John, written in the mid-second century, perhaps even slightly before AD150, mentions the name of John in the title. Papyrus p75, with Luke and John, written at the end of the second century, more or less contemporary with Irenaeus and the Anti-Marcionite *Prologues*, mentions Luke in a postscript at the end of the Gospel, and John at the beginning of his. Matthew's name is mentioned in the papyri p64 and p67, actually two parts of one and the same papyrus, which also belongs to the second century.

These extant papyri are, however, not from scrolls. They are all from a period when the 'codex' had taken over from the scroll in Christian circles. And the codex, the predecessor of our modern book format, did have the necessary information, like modern books, on a title page or above the actual beginning of the text, and sometimes at the end too. In other words, the transition from scroll to codex would have been the period when the information about the authors 'travelled' from the outside to the inside of the books.

This period of change is as exciting as it is vital for the preservation of our information about Jesus and his first followers. It is the period when Christians were, for the first time, at the forefront in the development of the 'modern media'.

An early revolution

In the British Library there are over 328 miles of shelving, growing at a rate of eight miles every year, and the Board is considering the option of refusing to accept books of 'secondary importance', whatever that may mean. It is one of the six libraries in the UK which receive, under the copyright Act, one copy of every book printed in the UK each year.

Imagine the problems faced by a library if it were to deal with scrolls instead of proper books, manuscripts, maps and microfilms—twenty-seven different scrolls for the new Testament alone, thirty-nine more for the Old Testament, and this would just cover the *Bible* (a word which means 'books', incidentally—the plural of the Greek word 'biblion', book).

Libraries and bookshops were in fact quite common in the time of Jesus and before. The most famous library of antiquity was established in Alexandria in about 296BC. At its height, just before its destruction by fire in 48/47BC, it contained some 700,000 scrolls. The slightly later library at Pergamon held some 200,000 scrolls. Caesar, the man indirectly responsible for the destruction of the Alexandrian library (fire from some of his ships spread across to the buildings), planned the first public library in Rome, built in 39BC. In 28BC, Augustus inaugurated the library on the Palatine. These are only some of many examples. The most famous Christian library of the early centuries (established before AD313, when Christianity began to enjoy state protection and support) was Origen's library at Caesarea Maritima in Palestine, expanded to its maximum size by his most important successor, Eusebius, with some thirty thousand scrolls and codices.

There was a flourishing international book trade, and there were bookshops almost everywhere. Aristophanes, the Greek playwright, alludes to a whole quarter of the city of Athens taken over by booksellers in his comedy *The Birds*, first performed in 414BC. And the Roman philosopher Seneca, an exact contemporary of the first Christian generation, complained as early as around AD57: 'What is the use of countless books and libraries, whose owner can hardly in his whole life peruse even all the catalogues?'

This enormous number of words on nothing but scrolls was as inconvenient for the reader as for the librarian. One could not just open a scroll like a modern book, look at the table of contents, leaf through the pages, find the required passage, close it and put it back on the shelf. One would have to unroll it slowly, using both hands. At the end, one had to re-roll it carefully to 'close' it. Scrolls could sometimes be as long as eight metres or more (the fragmentary scroll of Plato's *Symposium*, found at Oxyrhynchus in Egypt, would have been 7.5 metres long, like the famous scroll of Isaiah found at Qumran; and the *Temple Scroll* from Qumran cave Eleven measures 8.6 metres). What was more, it was a waste of space and material. These scrolls were nearly always written on one side only—on the inside, as it were. There are a few exceptions, but they are always singled out as such: Juvenal's first satire, written in about AD98 is one example; and two classic examples are found in the Bible. In the book of Ezekiel he says: 'Then I looked, and I saw a hand stretched out to me. In it was a scroll, which he unrolled before me. On both sides of it were written words of lament and mourning and woe.' And the book of Revelation records: 'Then I saw in the right hand of him who sat on the throne a scroll with writing on both sides and sealed with seven seals.'

This last-quoted passage, from the New Testament book of Revelation, confirms one further observation which has recently been disputed by textual critics and New Testament scholars who have apparently ignored that reference in Revelation: the first Christian scribes did not use the 'book-type' codex straightaway. They initially continued in the tradition of their Jewish neighbours and pagan contemporaries and used the scroll. In fact, as late as AD180, when the the use of codex had indeed replaced that of scrolls among Christian scribes, particularly valuable texts were still preserved as scrolls. For example, in the *Acts of Peter*, Peter is described as 'rolling up' a scroll of the Gospel—and even if these *Acts* are more like a novel than a historical document, no novelist would think of inventing the usage of the scroll by the first Christians if they had not really been in use at the time. And, as we have seen, in the *Acts of the Scillitan Martyrs*, the books of the Law and Paul's letters are explicitly described as being held in a 'capsa', the container for scrolls, not for codices.

Of course, there were good reasons for the first Christians

to write on scrolls. The most important one was tactical. Until AD70 at least—that is, until the destruction of the Temple in Jerusalem—the Christians were sincerely intent on staying in close contact with their fellow Jews. They still went to the Temple, and the first thing Paul did wherever he went on his journeys was to visit the local synagogue. Assuming, as we may, that most, if not all, New Testament writings were written before AD70, it would have been stupid to come up with a new format (even if it had already existed), when it was so easy and natural to compare scroll to scroll, like with like. There were the five scrolls of the Torah, and there were the five scrolls of the Gospels and Acts. Early Christian artists have depicted just such a scene of comparison in the Roman catacombs. And the Jerusalem or Palestinian Talmud, a detailed commentary, compiled in the fifth century, on the Mishnah (an AD200 law code), confirms this Christian attitude from the Jewish point of view: there it says that the Christians had their books written in the same format as the Jews, so as to underline that they were on equal terms as far as the Law (the 'Torah') was concerned.

There is, however, only one extant fragment of a New Testament text on a scroll—the disputed Qumran fragment 7Q5 (Mark 6:52–53), which must have been written before AD68, when the Qumran caves were closed, and probably, to judge by the style of handwriting, even before AD50. We shall look into this and other Qumran fragments further on. Those scholars who do not accept this identification claim that all surviving New Testament fragments are from codices and that there is therefore no existing manuscript evidence for the use of scrolls by the very first Christians. This would contradict the unequivocal circumstantial evidence mustered above.

Evidently, however, Christian scribes did begin to use the codex (or book-form) very early on. One of our oldest extant codex fragments, the famous p52 at the John Rylands Library in Manchester, with John 18:31–33 on the front and John 18:37–38 on the back, is conveniently dated to about

AD125, but it can be shown that exactly the same style of handwriting was in use as early as the time of Domitian (AD81–86). And indeed, if one of the reasons for retaining the use of the scroll had come to an end with the destruction of the Temple in Jerusalem in AD70, or, perhaps, with the official and final condemnation of the Christians by the Jewish council at Jamnia, in around AD90, then the Christians were free to relinquish tactical considerations and to look for more practical formats for their writings, leaving the Jews themselves to continue to use scrolls for the Torah to this very day.

Some time after AD70, but not much later than about AD90, would be the time in which the Christians changed over from the scroll to the codex. In fact, we find a hint at the use of a 'precursor' to the codex in Paul's second letter to Timothy. 'When you come,' Paul writes to Timothy, 'bring the cloak that I left with Carpus at Troas, and my scrolls, especially the parchments.' Compare the same passage in the Revised English Bible: 'When you come, bring the cloak I left with Carpus at Troas, and the books, particularly my notebooks.' Let us hope that the recipient of the letter was not as uncertain of what was meant as its translators into English. That books, in those days, consisted of scrolls, we already know. But why the alternatives 'parchments' and 'notebooks'? The Greek word used here is 'tas membranas'. And it has been shown, most recently by C. H. Roberts and T. C. Skeat, that this word means parchment as well as notebook, that is, a parchment notebook.

Parchment, made from the skin of certain animals (mostly sheep and goats, but also antelopes and others), could be produced anywhere, rather than only in the very limited regions where the papyrus plant was cultivated (almost exclusively in upper Egypt). On the other hand, there were fewer suitable animals than papyrus plants, and the technical process by which parchment was made from skin was much more complex than that needed to produce writing material from the papyrus stem. So parchment was more costly and valuable. But it was also more durable and therefore particularly suited for notebooks used for frequent reference. The text could easily be washed off again for second or third use: the smooth surface of the parchment was much more convenient than the rougher one of the papyrus.

But could Paul's 'notebook' have been a scroll? Some of the earliest known examples of 'notebooks' are a combination of tablets, mostly made of wood, covered by a layer of wax and held together by cords passed through holes in the wood, or by clasps. Closed, such a notebook would already have looked quite similar to a modern book. And the technical term for such a notebook was in Latin a 'codex'. What, then, of Paul's notebook, the 'membranai'? This term is derived from the Latin technical term for parchment. It is interesting to note that there was no equivalent in Greek. Paul uses the Latin word in a Greek spelling. And he uses it in the plural. In the singular it was the word for the material used, but in the plural it meant the end product: a number of parchment leaves bound together rather like the waxed wooden tablets which used to be called 'codices' (the plural of 'codex'). This, at any rate, is what the literary evidence suggests: Horace in his *Art of Poetry* (written about 19BC) and Persius, in his third Satire (written in about AD55 or slightly later, and so of exactly the same period as Paul's letters) use 'membranae' in this sense.

A great advocate of the parchment codex—not merely as a notebook, but for proper literary texts, was the Roman poet Martial (around AD40–104). He does not use the word codex (as this was still more or less confined to bound wax tablets), but the way he uses 'membranae', in a poem dated to about AD84–86, shows that he has books in mind. It seems that there were, at this time, parchment codices of writings by authors such as Homer, Virgil, Cicero and Livy. But the codices were uncommon and without a real 'market'. Martial tries his best to convince his readers that they should patronize the codex, since it is much more handy than the scroll for travelling and much more economical for one's library. It has been suggested that Martial's idea was the 'pocket book', the 'paperback' of his day. But Martial and his innovative publisher, Secundus, failed in their marketing attempt. In his later poems, the concept does not reappear, and none of the major authors following on from Martial, not even those, such as Pliny the Younger, who specifically discuss the subject of writing and publishing, refer to their having knowledge—let alone use—of the parchment codex. A single parchment codex written in Martial's lifetime has survived: a fragment from an otherwise unknown *History of the Macedonian Wars*, dated to the late first century AD. It is now on display in the British Library (Papyrus DCCXLV).

In late first- and early second-century Rome, the old conventions prevailed. It was left to absolute outsiders, if not outcasts—the Christians—to develop the format unhindered among themselves, and only after it had firmly established itself in their own circles, bookshops and libraries was it finally adopted in Graeco-Roman society—and in publishing generally.

On the basis of the evidence I have drawn on here, the 'membranai' referred to in Paul's letter cannot have been complete books. The juxtaposition of 'books' ('biblia') and 'notebooks' ('membranai') in 2 Timothy 4:13, suggests two different types of text. The 'books' are proper literary texts, possibly a combination of Old Testament scripture and classical Greek literature. For example, in another of Paul's letters, to Titus, the Greek philosophers Epimenides and Callimachus are quoted (Titus 1:2—Epimenides *On Oracles*; Callimachus *On Zeus*), together with Christian writings such as Mark's Gospel (Mark is actually mentioned in 2 Timothy). As for the mention of 'membranai', we are led to assume that this does mean notebooks which could thus be drafts of letters, excerpts from other texts, memos and the like. If 2 Timothy was written by Paul while under house arrest in Rome, such a request would make sense: his books and notebooks—all the writing material which would have been vital to him while he was teaching as intensively as he was, for we read in the book of Acts, chapter 28, verses 30–31: 'For two whole years Paul stayed there in his own rented house and welcomed all who came to see him. Boldly he preached the kingdom of God and taught about the Lord Jesus Christ.'

Paul, then, was not the inventor of the codex in the innovative form given to it later by the early Christians. What he used was a well-established precursor, the parchment notebook. But soon afterwards, some time after AD70 or AD90 at the latest, as we have seen, the Christians did begin to revolutionize the history of book production. (It was the first Christian publishing revolution; the second coming with Gutenberg in 1456, when the first complete book, a Bible, was printed using movable type.) And, from the start, they did something which probably contributed to the eventual triumph of the codex over the scroll, as much as anything else: instead of the valuable and expensive parchment, they used the cheaper if less elegant and durable papyrus, which they had already used for their scrolls.

But what led the early Christians to use the codex? Several reasons suggest themselves. One has already been mentioned. After the destruction of the Temple and the condemnation of the Christians by the Jews assembled at Jamnia, the break between (Jewish) Christians and Jews was complete. There was no longer any need to be seen to be 'on a par' with the Jews; on the contrary, it may even have been thought advisable to demonstrate the break by switching to a conspicuously different text format. A second reason was the one which would have become more and more important as the number of missionary journeys increased and writings were transported by messengers: the codex was not only handier, smaller, and more economical, with writing on *both* sides of a leaf; it could contain, say, the five historical books of the Gospels and Acts, or a collection of Paul's letters, in one sizeable 'book', instead of five or more different scrolls. The practicality of this would also have become apparent in times of persecution: how much easier to hide a book or two than a whole 'capsa' full of scrolls.

Also, Christians would have used copies of the Old Testament, in the Greek Septuagint version: thirty-nine books, quite a few of them longer than any New Testament writing. For these, the advantages of the codex soon became equally apparent. The main purpose of copying, collecting and using these Old Testament texts (apart from providing historical information) was to be able to quote, make cross references and point to Old Testament prophecies fulfilled in Christ. Therefore, the book-type codices, which one could leaf through at ease, made the actual use of the texts in teaching, preaching, studying and commenting much easier (at that time the system of chapter and verse numbering had not been invented). Compare the scroll to a modern microfilm roll, and you will realize how difficult it must have been, prior to the codex, to find exact passages quickly, to refer back and forth at ease.

Jesus himself, in Luke, chapter 4, solemnly unrolls a scroll of Isaiah, reads from it, and rolls it up again: 'Then he rolled up the scroll, gave it back to the attendant and sat down. The eyes of everyone in the synagogue were fastened on him, and he said to them, "Today this scripture is fulfilled in your hearing."' It is almost surprising that such an awe-inspiring precedent, or the equally magnificent scene of the scroll with the seven seals in the book of Revelation did not persuade the early Christians of the inherent 'holiness' of the scroll: 'The sky receded like a scroll, rolling up, and every mountain and island was removed from its place' (Revelation 6:14).

It is a sign of the Christians' 'freedom in Christ Jesus' (Galatians 2:4) that they did not do so. They took Jesus' great commission to go out into the world and preach the gospel so seriously that they carried through the change to the use of the codex not least because it helped them to 'make disciples of all nations'.

5
Controversies Over Ancient Manuscripts

'Some circumstantial evidence is very strong,' the Canadian novelist Henry David Thoreau once wrote, 'as when you find a trout in the milk.' It is a situation often encountered by historians of new Testament times; and with it go some unrelenting questions. Is it really a trout? What type of milk is it? Who produced the milk and who put the trout (if it is a trout) in it? Why? How? When? Where?

Papyrus: the priceless treasure

Some scholars say that New Testament papyrus fragments have been found among the Dead Sea Scrolls at Qumran. Are they really New Testament fragments? What type of cave is it? Who collected the manuscripts in that cave, and who placed the New Testament texts (if they are New Testament texts) in it? Why? How? When? Where (and where from)? We shall look into this particular riddle soon.

There are, to this day, ninety-six known papyrus fragments generally accepted as parts of the New Testament—the very earliest, oldest textual evidence of New Testament writings. Scholars world-wide are working on further fragments and I have myself edited one such fragment quite recently, the so-called p73, or Bodmer L, of the sixth century, with two passages from the Gospel of Matthew. It is detective work, painstaking, slow, but ideally

71

immensely rewarding. Of course, everyone is hoping for new, important discoveries, comparable to the sensational Dead Sea Scrolls.

There are whole boxes full of unedited fragments in Vienna. Will any of them turn out to be a very early New Testament papyrus? The slow process of editing the manuscripts found at Herculaneum, that Italian town destroyed together with Pompeii by the eruption of Vesuvius in AD79 keeps everyone in suspense: will there be exciting new discoveries eventually? Archaeologists know about the traces of a cross found on the wall of a house in Herculaneum. Christians were there, and obviously before AD79. Did they read Paul's letters or the Gospels? Could fragments of such texts still be among the unedited, unpublished finds?

And then again: do we want to know? After all, we have our English translations, and there are editions of the Greek New Testament with all the paraphernalia of scholarship. I remember a sticker once very popular in certain circles in Germany: 'We do not need nuclear power,' it said, 'we get our electricity straight out of the socket.' Somehow the electricity had to get to the socket in the first place, so did the material assembled in Greek New Testament editions and used for all modern translations. The text had a long journey—it had to be assembled, scrutinized, evaluated. A formidable task even if all we had were those ninety-six fragments.

In fact, there are more than 5,400 ancient and early medieval manuscripts of the whole or parts of the New Testament. And although some 95 per cent belong to a particular, more or less coherent group, known as the Byzantine or Majority text, every single one of them may be important and must not be overlooked. One is led by the assumption, so often proved correct, that even relatively 'young' manuscripts may be more important than some of the oldest. A younger manuscript may well preserve traces of an extremely reliable textual tradition which is older than the oldest existing manuscript known at present. It is one of the continuous tasks of the scholar to establish which manuscript is the best, has the fewest errors, represents the most reliable tradition. This sounds complicated, and sometimes it is very complicated indeed.

The classical philologist Paul Maas tried to explain it like this (with apologies for the sexist language): 'The (textual) witnesses are related to the original somewhat as the descendants of a man are related to their ancestor. One might perhaps illustrate the transmission of errors along the same lines by treating all females as sources of error.'

Maas then tries again, and comes up with the following comparison: 'A river comes from an inaccessible source under the peak of a high mountain. It divides underground, its branches divide further, and some of these branches then come to the surface on the mountainside as springs; the water of these springs at once drains away and may come to the surface at several places farther down the mountainside and finally flows onward in visible form overground. The water from its source onwards is of ever-changing but fine and pure colours. In its subterranean course it flows past several places at which colouring matters from time to time dissolve into the water; the same thing happens every time the stream divides and every time it comes to the surface in the spring. Every influx changes the colour of a certain part of the stream, and this part keeps the colour permanently; only very slight colour changes are eliminated by natural processes. The distinction between the dyed water and the original remains always visible to the eye, but only occasionally in the sense that the eye at once recognizes as falsified by influxes; often only in the sense that the difference between the colours of the various springs is discernible. On the other hand, the falsified elements can often be detected and the original colour restored by chemical methods; at other times this method fails. The object of the investigation is to test the genuineness of the colours on the evidence of the springs.'

I have quoted from this study so extensively not least for one illuminating reason: here is one of the great textual critics of the twentieth century, writing for other textual critics, and yet he has to resort to female errors, rivers and colours to explain the intricacies of textual traditions. And with all this, they still sound as complicated as they are in reality!

Spare a thought for Erasmus of Rotterdam, though. When he edited the Greek New Testament at Basle in 1517, he produced what is still regarded as the first printed edition of the Greek text—although the text known as the Complutensian Polyglot, printed in Spain, was ready three years earlier but was prevented from publication by Pope Leo X because he was waiting for the return of valuable manuscripts. The Spaniards, it is said, did have some of the best manuscripts at their disposal; not so poor Erasmus.

Erasmus, one of the outstanding scholars of the sixteenth century, was forced to make do with a mere four manuscripts, one for Acts with Epistles, one for Revelation, two for the Gospels. None of them was older than the twelfth century, all belonged to the same type of manuscript (the Byzantine or Majority Text), and none of them was one of those papyri so proudly placed at the top of each list of New Testament manuscripts today. Worse still, Erasmus' manuscript of Revelation, which he had borrowed from a German friend, Johannes Reuchlin, did not include the last few verses, 22:16–21. Erasmus simply 'retranslated' these verses from the Latin version of the Bible, the Vulgate, back into Greek. Small wonder then that some words in these verses never occurred in any 'real' Greek manuscripts of these verses, many of which have been discovered since.

Erasmus' version remained influential for centuries, and some of his more peculiar Greek structures and 'corrections' found their way, via translation, into the most widespread English Bible, the Authorized Version or King James' Bible of 1611. This was mainly based on Erasmus' Greek text and its successors (known, in its standardized form, as the *Textus Receptus*, the commonly received text).

A classic example of such well-meant corruption of the text occurs in Acts 9:6. Paul's question on the road to Damascus,

74

'And he trembling and astonished said, Lord what wilt thou have me do?', is not known from any extant Greek manuscript; Erasmus added it from the Latin Vulgate which he had in front of him. Today, of course, it is no longer included in critical editions of the Latin Bible (you will find a reference to it in the notes), and new English translations do not have it either.

Two positive conclusions can be drawn from the case of Erasmus: first, it was possible to work with the Greek New Testament even when there were no papyri and only a handful of manuscripts available. People made do with what they had, and the general quality of their work, not least in the early editions of Estienne in Paris (1550) and Beza in Geneva (1565) is quite remarkable. We may have by far the better editions of the Greek New Testament today, based on more than 5,400 manuscripts, but the sheer courage and ingenuity of those scholars who worked with a mere handful of them demand our greatest respect. Second, even though practically all the manuscripts used for these early editions belonged to the Byzantine or Majority Text, relegated to second rank by modern scholars, serious attempts have recently been made to demonstrate that this group of manuscripts deserves renewed attention as a witness to a textual tradition which is important and informative in its own right.

Behind all this lies the plain fact that no *original* manuscript of any New Testament writing has survived. Why not? There is, by definition, always only one original manuscript. But people in antiquity did not necessarily regard an original as uniquely valuable. A manuscript was used and re-used until it fell apart, and then a new copy was made while the old one was discarded. In fact, a place where one of the largest finds of manuscripts was made, Oxyryhnchus in upper Egypt, was nothing but a dumping ground for discarded documents, letters and literary texts.

Add to this the fact that only a very few texts were actually handwritten by the authors themselves. Look at Paul's letters. We read at the end of the letter to the Romans: 'I, Tertius, who wrote down this letter, greet you in the Lord.' Paul specifically points out the exception made where parts of letters are written in his own hand. For example, in Galatians 6:11: 'See what large letters I use as I write to you with my own hand!' Or Colossians 4:18: 'I, Paul, write this greeting in my own hand.' (Incidentally, this last quotation is a brilliant example of authenticity: there is Paul, in prison, reading the letter as written down by his secretary, Timothy probably— see Colossians 1:1; he wants to sign it, and feels how his chains distract him, rattling on the desk. And on the spur of the moment, he adds: 'Remember my chains. Grace be with you.'—and so the letter ends.) There are two more examples: 'I, Paul, write this greeting in my own hand, which is the distinguishing mark in all my letters. This is how I write.' and 'I, Paul, write this greeting in my own hand,' found in 2 Thessalonians 3:17 and 1 Corinthians 16:21.

Persecution after persecution was meted out on the Christian communities until the age of Constantine the Great in the fourth century AD. And one of the avowed aims of such waves of persecution was the destruction of Christian writings. Many originals will have perished like this. In fact, even when Christianity enjoyed state protection, manuscripts could have been destroyed by later invaders— the Visigoths, the Ostrogoths, the Vandals (the original ones), and others. We know that Emperor Constantine ordered his court librarian and historian Eusebius to have fifty codices of the Greek Bible copied for him, well-executed, valuable 'court editions'. And yet not a single one of them has survived. Some of them may simply have perished through natural decay, or neglect, or accidental destruction by fire, and so on. All the early manuscripts which we have come from the few places where they enjoyed natural protection: the dry sands of Egypt, the caves of Qumran, the arid climate of Sinai, the lava layers of Herculaneum, dried up bindings of mummies.

Rightly or wrongly, papyri have become the priceless

treasures of classical scholarship, and whatever else may be said about their importance, it remains true that the oldest extant New Testament papyri are also the oldest New Testament documents. They are older than the parchment codices, the 'uncial' and 'minuscule' manuscripts of later centuries which are sometimes of the greatest value as far as the text which they preserve is concerned.

But papyri were not always held in such high esteem. When a theologian called Grynaeus gave the first two papyri to the library at Basle in the late 1500s, no one paid any attention to them, until they were finally published in 1917, four-and-a-half centuries later. Or put yourself in the place of that antiquarian who, in 1778, bought a documentary papyrus scroll of the second century AD from some Egyptian peasants and then watched as they happily burnt fifty more scrolls, enjoying the aromatic fragrance of the smoke. Or take another example, first told by the German theologian Adolf Deissmann in 1909. A Turkish peasant had found, while ploughing, an earthenware jar with a book. Not knowing what to do with it, he went to the village teacher who told him to throw it into the water. However, the following year, when the water level of the lake receded, someone else found the jar with the book. This time, the teacher said: '- Throw it into the fire.' And thus the book was finally destroyed.

In Deissmann's anecdote, it was a parchment book. Papyri and parchments often suffered the same fate as long as people did not suspect their real value and were perhaps— occasionally at least—afraid of something uncanny, evil in such uncommon finds, as the teacher in that anecdote probably was. Worse still, even Christian monks, as late as the nineteenth century, did not always know what they were doing. Konstantin von Tischendorf tells the story of how he discovered the famous Codex Sinaiticus at St Catherine's monastery in the Sinai in 1844 (most of which, 347 leaves, are now in the British Library, with 43 leaves still in Leipzig, three in Leningrad, and twelve recently discovered leaves still at the monastery). He noticed some parchment leaves in a basket, ready to be burned in the stove, where two full baskets had already been destroyed—as the monks happily told him when he could not conceal his horror. That basket which he saw contained a stack of leaves from what still is one of the two oldest codices of the whole Greek Bible. An hour later, and it too would have been burnt, like so many other papyri and parchments we do not even know about.

Von Tischendorf himself only included one papyrus in one of his critical editions of the New Testament, the p11—a late, seventh-century papyrus, now at the Leningrad State Public Library, with parts of 1 Corinthians. Only eight further papyri were known about by the end of the nineteenth century, anyhow: not many, compared to the ninety-six we know of today.

The real breakthrough happened between 1933 and 1935. In 1933, Sir Frederick Kenyon published the papyrus codex p45, thirty leaves with large parts of the Gospels and Acts, and datable to the late second century. A year later, he published the papyrus codex p46, eighty-six leaves with most of Paul's letters, and with Hebrews, but without 2 Thessalonians and the 'Pastoral Epistles' (1 and 2 Timothy and Titus). Generally dated to around AD200, it may well be—according to the papyrologist Young Kyu Kim—late first century, only some thirty years after the death of Paul. And then, in 1935, the most famous of them all was published—C. H. Roberts' edition of the p52, Papyrus Ryl.Greek 457, which was found among a hoard of papyri at the John Rylands Library, Manchester, containing John 18:31–33 and 18:37–38. Dated to around AD125, but perhaps up to thirty years older and falling within the lifetime of the evangelist himself, it is still commonly regarded as the oldest known fragment of a New Testament text. (Its new rival, the Qumran fragment 7Q5, first edited in 1962, and first identified in 1972, will be discussed later.)

Papyri have fascinated scholars and the general public alike ever since. Other finds, such as the near-complete codex of John's Gospel, the p66 or Bodmer II, at the Bibliotheca Bodmeriana in Cologny near Geneva, published in 1956 and dateable to around AD150, or the p72 (Bodmer XVII-IXX), an early third-century codex containing, among other texts, the oldest known papyrus manuscript of 1 and 2 Peter and Jude, all added to the excitement about the sudden growth in early documents. All of them were written, after all, while Christianity was still a minority religion, threatened with persecution of its followers and the destruction of its manuscripts, a hundred years and more before the beginnings of a Christian publishing industry under Emperor Constantine.

We have become used to these facts and figures. But let us keep in mind how extraordinary they are: there is nothing like it in non-Christian literature of antiquity. Last year in Jerusalem, I met Joseph Geiger, a classical philologist who was in the process of editing a papyrus find of unique importance together with his colleague, Hannah M. Cotton. At the fortress of Masada, archaeologists had found a papyrus fragment of Virgil's epic poem, the *Aeneid*. Virgil, who lived from 70–19BC, was one of the most important poets of the Roman Empire, and his influence on European literature throughout the Middle Ages was beyond compare. One of his poems, known as the fourth eclogue, was even regarded as a prophecy of Christ's birth, and there is a statue of him in the Spanish Cathedral of Zamorra, right next to the Old Testament prophets. And yet, early manuscripts of his writings are extremely scarce.

This papyrus from Masada, probably left there by one of the occupying Roman soldiers in or soon after AD73, is now the oldest papyrus of any work by Virgil ever found. It contains just one line from the *Aeneid*. That is all there is, and yet it is uniquely important for anyone interested in Virgil. And look at the date again: about AD73, that is, some ninety-two years after Virgil's death, when he left the *Aeneid* unfinished.

Other examples of the distance between the origin of the

work and the oldest known manuscript abound for non-Christian literature; perhaps the most illuminating is the case of Homer, the unrivalled father of epic poetry. The oldest known complete manuscript of his works belongs to the thirteenth century, in other words, at least 2000 years after the lifetime of the author. Tacitus, the Roman historian, does not fare much better: for the first six books of his *Annals* we depend on a single manuscript discovered in 1510.

In the previous chapter, we saw that Christian scribes and historians did their best to safeguard their knowledge about the authorship of the first Christian writings. Here, we have seen that the actual textual tradition is unique in its closeness to the original texts, and the sheer number of texts which have survived. In itself, none of this 'proves' anything. But it once again shows that people were conscious of the uncommon character of the documents they possessed, and that they did their best, with all their human shortcomings, to propagate and multiply from the beginning the evidence contained in the written gospel, the 'good news' meant to be read by everyone.

6

Dating the Fragments

'Mystarion to his own Stotoetis: many greetings!

I sent my right-hand man Blastos to you, since I need two-pronged sticks for my olive gardens. Do not hold him up: you know that I need him as soon as possible. Farewell.

Eleventh Year of Tiberius Claudius Caesar Augustus Germanicus Emperor, in the month Sebastos 15.'

Anyone who has ever walked through the olive groves of Tuscany in the late summer will understand this letter. However, as the date at the end tells us, it was not written yesterday or last week, but on 12 September, AD50. New Testament times. One year earlier, the same Claudius had expelled Jews and (Jewish) Christians from Rome. At Corinth, Luke writes in Acts 18:2, Paul 'met a Jew named Aquila, a native of Pontus, who had recently come from Italy with his wife Priscilla, because Claudius had ordered all the Jews to leave Rome.'

This letter by Mystarion, sent to his dear Stotoetis, bears a precise date, 12 September 50 (according to our modern calendar). And we know the whereabouts of the *original* of this letter—it is at the former Royal Museums Berlin (now State Museums), where it was first edited in 1898.

A dated original manuscript, with day, month and year—this is what one needs time and again. Why? Because otherwise it would not be possible to determine the time or period of origin of *un*dated manuscripts. By comparing the styles of writing, individual letters as well as overall characteristics, one is able to place a document to within some twenty, thirty years of its actual date: in antiquity, these features were much more constant (and remained so for longer) than they are today.

And the importance of all this? *No early New Testament papyrus or parchment is dated.* This should not come as a surprise—only legal or official documents and original personal letters would normally have been dated in those times. The oldest firmly dated manuscript of any biblical writing is in fact a parchment codex kept in the British Library (and occasionally put on display), the Syriac Peshitta version of Genesis and Exodus, dated to the year 775 of the Greek era, that is, AD463–464. The oldest dated New Testament manuscript is a Greek parchment minuscule of AD835, containing the Gospels, and kept at the Leningrad Public Library.

But if none of the earliest manuscripts, none of the highly respected papyri of the New Testament is dated, then how can one say that they really are early and belong to a certain period? You may have noticed, in the previous chapter, that such datings are not undisputed: a case in point is the papyrus codex p46, commonly dated to around AD200, but now seriously judged, thanks to new material, to be late first century. Datings can, and do, differ. And one yardstick providing at least some degree of certainty is comparison with dated manuscripts. Thus, any manuscripts looking very similar to the one with Mystarion's letter to Stotoetis could be dated to the period around AD50, give or take a decade or two.

Just suppose for a moment that Jesus had written not 'on the ground with his finger' (John 8:6), but on a papyrus 'with pen and ink' (3 John 13), and suppose that someone were to claim to have found this very papyrus: a comparative analysis of styles of handwriting would determine fairly quickly if such a papyrus could at least fall within the lifetime of Jesus.

Sometimes, though, scholars hesitate to face the potential consequences of such comparisons. The famous p52 of John's Gospel in John Rylands Library, Manchester, is commonly dated to around AD125, but may be up to three decades older. The reason for such a wide margin lies in the material used for comparison in the evaluation of the papyrus. C. H. Roberts, the editor of the p52, had drawn upon several dated papyri, among them one from AD94, another from AD127 and another from the reign of Domitian, AD81–96. Opting for around AD125 thus means that around AD90 would at least be as plausible. But imagine the consequences of a verdict in favour of AD90: suddenly, all those who prefer a dating of the Gospel of John prior to AD70 would have an important ally. P52 is a copy, it was found in Egypt and thus presupposes a considerably earlier original. Better play safe and prefer the later date, rather than encourage those reckless early daters!

C. H. Roberts, it is true, did not have such qualms. When he published his edition, there were quite a few New Testament scholars around who thought that John's Gospel was written in the last quarter of the *second* century. Even a 'conservative' papyrus dating of AD125 would put paid to such fantasies. But present-day textual critics should at least be prepared to state openly that p52 *could* be even older still, dangerously close to the lifetime of the Gospel's author.

Making comparisons is the tool of the trade which enabled Young Kyu Kim to propose that the codex of Paul's writings p46 is late first century rather than around AD200; and comparisons will influence much of the work to be done in future. But, as we have seen, there are limits to the accuracy of this method. So what can one do if one wants to know even more about the exact date and origin of a given manuscript?

Are there forgeries?

Occasionally, it has been suggested by ill-informed controversialists that the Gospels in their present state are 'purified' fabrications of later centuries, with an invented picture of a Jesus who never existed like this, if he ever existed at all. Gerald Messadié's bestselling novel *L'homme qui devint Dieu*, first published in 1988, ends with an 'academic' epilogue in which the author, assistant editor-in-chief of a scientific magazine, claims that some of the most important elements of the Gospels are inventions; and he is only imitating what others have tried before him. The most notorious of these, perhaps, was G. A. Wells, a professor of German at Birkbeck College, London, who managed to distort the evidence until he reached the conclusion that Jesus never existed at all. And the middle ground is occupied by those who make their own selections about what they think can be true and what must be wrong, from the virgin birth to the empty tomb. As someone once said, 'We know that Jesus died, but was he ever born?'

Obviously, the better, earlier, and more reliable our sources, the easier it is to rule out claims of inventions, forgeries, illegitimate additions. And there is a temptation to get carried away in the process of establishing the oldest texts with definite dates. The most ingenious example was provided by a highly gifted Greek scholar, Constantine Simonides, who was inclined to write some 'ancient biblical manuscripts' himself. But he did also provide undoubtedly authentic material. This included, among others, some important leaves of the *Shepherd of Hermas*, a colourful, visionary text of early Christianity, of the so-called Apostolic Fathers, usually dated to around AD150, but which is probably considerably older (John A. T. Robinson suggested AD85 or earlier).

Other authentic manuscripts provided by Simonides are still at the British Library. However, Simonides' unreliability and his whimsical approach made it quite difficult to believe in anything he offered, including his most sensational claim, the find of fragments from a first-century manuscript of the Gospel of Matthew which he published in 1861. According to one of these papyri, the

84

Gospel was written by the deacon Nicolaos, at the behest of Matthew, in the *fifteenth* year after the Ascension. Since 7 April AD30 is the most probable date of the crucifixion, and since Jesus was with the disciples for forty days after the resurrection (Acts 1:3), 19 May AD30 is the probable date of the Ascension. The date of the Gospel would be some time in AD45 on this basis.

The riddle of these fragments Simonides referred to remains unsolved: they have been categorically refuted by classical scholars and New Testament critics alike, but Simonides cannot have written them himself. They belonged to the private collection of Joseph Mayor in Liverpool, and Simonides had simply obtained permission to read them, which he did at the library of Mayor, most of the time in the presence of the owner and other people. Only after the 'discovery' of these fragments of Matthew's Gospel had been made did Simonides take some of them to his flat.

If they are forgeries, Simonides cannot be the forger, but since his credibility is practically non-existent, no one has been prepared to re-investigate the whole affair. It has been laid to rest among the extravagances of the nineteenth century. Scholars such as Bernard Orchard and Harold Riley who think that Matthew could have been written before AD45 might think it fun to have a closer look at the material again, some 125 years after the end of the original debate. (Keith Elliott of Leeds University recently re-examined one of Simonides' other claims: that he himself had written the Codex Sinaiticus which Konstantin von Tischendorf found at St. Catherine's Monastery!)

Such 'revivals', when they happen, occasionally reveal surprising news about real or alleged forgeries. Last year, a scholar from Giessen University, Petra Halder-Sinn, and Hannes Lehmann from Freiburg looked again at one of the big scandals of archaeology, the case of the Fibula Praenestina. A fibula is a brooch or 'safety pin', and this one is special since it is not only very old (seventh century BC), but is made from gold, 10.7 centimetres long and inscribed with the oldest known text of anything written in the Latin language. 'Manios med fhefhaked Numasioi,' it reads, 'Manois made me for Numasios'. Found in a tomb in Praeneste (modern Palestrina in Italy), details of it were published in 1887 by Wolfgang Helbig, of the German Archaeological Institute in Rome, and it was immediately hailed as a sensation. And so it remained until the Italian epigraphist Margherita Guarducci came along in 1980, and claimed that Helbig had written the text himself: a forgery, 'il mostro della Prenestina', as the Italian press called it, the monster of the Fibula Praenestina.

Guarducci had mainly relied on a graphological analysis which apparently proved the identity of both handwritings— Helbig's and the one on the fibula—as being one and the same. To anyone who has ever seen the fibula or photographic reproductions of it, this is patent nonsense. The style of the inscription, authentic or not, is so different from Helbig's or any other nineteenth-century hand that 'proof' is simply not possible either way. If it is a forgery, it must have been a very clever forger—for only recently—one hundred years or so after Helbig's discovery—have further comparable inscriptions been found. These confirm the linguistic and palaeographical characteristics of the fibula inscription. Ms Halder-Sinn's reassessment has initiated the rehabilitation of Wolfgang Helbig and of the fibula, which will now be analyzed again, this time with the latest technical and chemical means.

In a paper published four years ago, Anton Fackelmann claimed that he had identified fragments of a first version of Mark's Gospel on a papyrus from the breastplate binding of an Egyptian mummy found in 1972. It was a palimpsest (a manuscript on which at least two, in this case at least four, successive texts had been written, each one erased, scraped or washed off to make room for the next). As the author of the article admitted, an exact reading was not possible in spite of different photographic techniques. Anyone who has seen the photographs will readily agree. And even the text he does claim to be able to read is not even remotely related to Mark. However, he went on to date the papyrus to 'at the latest the second half of the first century', because the Ptolemaic style of handwriting cannot be found after the second half of the second century, and also because the way the glue was applied to attach it to the mummy's binding was discontinued after the Ptolemaic epoch. This insistence on the Ptolemaic period is yet another problem, though, for it actually ended in 30BC, and no one would want to claim that first drafts of Mark's Gospel were written some twenty to thirty years before Jesus was born!

Such examples, whether the Matthew fragment of Simonides or the proto-Mark of Fackelmann, demonstrate the lengths to which some people have gone to find or produce evidence of New Testament manuscripts written at a very early date. Sound scepticism is a safeguard here. And it is a safeguard against the opposite claims, of those who want to detract from the indisputable strength of the early gospel evidence as we have seen in previous chapters.

There is always the possibility of new discoveries. After all, in the past there have been incidents when a new papyrus was found or deciphered unexpectedly—like the p52 of John's Gospel which no one could have *expected* to find at the John Rylands Library, University of Manchester, nor that it was of such an early date. So it cannot be absolutely ruled out that one day a copy of Paul's short and personal letter to Philemon will be found, *with* the date at the end, as in Mystarion's letter to Stotoetis. Or a copy of Paul's lost letter to the Laodiceans (see Colossians 4:16). Or of Clement of Alexandria's late second-century commentary on 2 Peter, a copy of which we know still existed in the ninth-century library of the Byzantine scholar Photius.

All this may sound fanciful and does not gain scholarly respectability when, for example, we read the best-selling novel by Umberto Eco *The Name of the Rose*, which focuses on the crimes committed for the sake of the lost second book of Aristotle's Poetics, the part on 'comedy', which no one thought existed any more. It is discovered (in the fictional world) that a copy is kept at the library of a monastery—which is then, of course, burnt when the library goes up in flames at the end.

Such stories about lost or found manuscripts, secret messages and passages, unheard-of insights into the wisdom of the world or the truth behind beloved stories always make good copy. And public attention is easily won with the cry of scandal or intrigue. Only quite recently, it has once again been claimed that the reason why many Dead Sea Scrolls have still not been published some forty years after their discovery is their devastating contents—disproving the New Testament accounts or damaging to the historico-political position of the modern state of Israel. Of course, this is blatant nonsense, even though the sober truth is almost as frustrating: until recently, too few scholars were working with too many extremely difficult manuscript fragments and doing too many other things besides.

Sometimes, texts are 'sensationally' found which never even existed. Visitors to the Holy Land may have been to the Monastery of Mar Saba, south east of Jerusalem. A place in the middle of nowhere, quiet, timeless. I once stood on the ridge of the wadi, the dry rocky water course, looking down at it and into the desert, lost in thought, when suddenly a jet fighter plane broke the sound barrier overhead. It was, in the truest sense of the word, an earth-shattering experience, with war and peace meeting there in two of their symbols. At Mar Saba, a monastery established in 482, Morton Smith claims to have discovered a copy of a letter written by Clement of Alexandria to a certain Theodorus, containing quotes from a 'secret gospel' of Mark. Smith made his 'discovery' in 1958, and no one has since seen the original of the seventeenth-century edition of Ignatius' letters to which this document is said to have been appended. All that is available to the rest of the scholarly community are photographs.

It is a strange story indeed: the codex of Ignatius' letters was dated 1646. Apparently, the original of the letter of

Clement of Alexandria (who lived from around AD150 to around AD219) still existed at that time for a copy of it to be made. Or was it a copy of a copy? In any case, the original has disappeared without trace, together with the original of the codex, since Smith discovered it. It took him fifteen years to publish his find, accompanying it with quite far-fetched theories: that the two quotations from the 'secret gospel' of Mark contained in Clement's letters are based on the Aramaic original, which was the source of the Gospels of Mark and John. He also claimed that the quotations described the true, historical Jesus, a man of sexual licentiousness with certain homosexual tendencies, a magician whose picture was falsified by James, his brother, and by Paul. In the letter, 'Clement' is at least made out to dissociate himself from some of the more explicit statements of the so-called 'secret gospel'. But the whole thing is ridiculous enough to be laughed out of court.

It is all too good to be true, anyhow. This seventeenth-century manuscript copy is free from the writing errors typical of the textual tradition of the time: a spotless copy, tailor-made. And even the alleged quotations from Mark's 'secret gospel' are too Markan to be Mark, as has been observed by analysts; a forger's attempt to overreach himself, to improve on the real thing. Considerable doubt must be cast on the existence of such a letter of Clement of Alexandria, and even more so on the existence of a second, 'secret' version of Mark's Gospel written by the evangelist. And if such a secret gospel existed after all and was somehow known to the real Clement of Alexandria, it cannot have been anything but a characteristically late gnostic concoction, datable to the mid-second century at the earliest and worthless as a source of information about the historical Jesus.

The Essene connection

The single most hotly disputed New Testament discovery

was made in 1972, and its consequences would take us right back to the fifties of the first century, a mere twenty years or so after the death and resurrection of Jesus.

What happened? A Spanish papyrologist, José O'Callaghan, suggested that one of the caves with the Dead Sea Scrolls, the seventh cave at Qumran, contained New Testament fragments, among them parts of the Gospel of Mark. Since the Qumran caves were closed in AD68, and since the particular fragment suggested to be Mark 6:52–53 had been dated, prior to its identification, to a period ending in AD50, O'Callaghan's thesis was truly hair-raising. The whole question of the dating of the Gospels was brought into focus. A papyrus fragment of Mark's Gospel *earlier* than AD68, perhaps earlier than AD50? Impossible, of course.

Not only this—Qumran was the 'monastery' of the Essenes, an extreme Jewish group, and how on earth could Christian documents have found their way to the library— and later to the caves—of this strictly regulated, autonomous, closely-knit community? Again, impossible. True enough, those fragments from the seventh cave were very small, and their identification depended on painstaking, detailed analysis—but hardly anyone was prepared to give the identification the benefit of the doubt, since the opinion was: in view of the historical situation, these fragments simply *could not* be parts of the New Testament. Or could they? Since 1984, the debate has been re-opened, with new material, further details, and, not least, the helpful corollaries of new historical and archaeological insights into the contacts between Christians and Essenes at the time of Jesus and immediately afterwards.

Let us look, on the basis of the most recent research, at the life of the Essene community in the time of Jesus. As we already know, neither Jesus nor his followers lived in a cultural vacuum. They were part of a multi-faceted society. And the New Testament, even though it was not meant to be read like a sociological study, offers many glimpses into the lives of a wide variety of peoples, tribes, and factions. There are the Pharisees, the Sadducees, the Zealots, the Samaritans, the Syro-Phoenicians, the Hellenists, the Romans—the lot. Only the Essenes are missing from among the main groups known to have populated Palestine at the time of Jesus. Or so it seems. It is true that we do not find their name mentioned in the New Testament. Indeed, they did not call themselves Essenes, the name was given to them by first-century 'outsiders' such as Josephus and Pliny.

There are, however, tell-tale signs of their existence, and of their very early contacts with Jesus and the disciples: contacts that later may have become quite useful in the tradition and safekeeping of the earliest Christian documents. Needless to say, this is not going to become a revival of the old 'Jesus was an Essene' stories, long and conclusively refuted. Close contacts, behaving in a neighbourly way, or even learning from one another do not amount to copy-cat behaviour or identical origins.

In fact, in the New Testament we find the first traces of the Essenes recorded in the account of the last days of Jesus in Jerusalem. 'Where do you want us to go and make preparations for you to eat the Passover?' the disciples ask him. He sends two of them to go into the city, 'and a man carrying a pot of water will meet you. Follow him. Say to the owner of the house he enters, "The Teacher asks: Where is my guest room, where I may eat the Passover with my disciples?" He will show you a large upper room, furnished and ready. Make preparations for us there.' (Mark 14:12–15)

In those days, water was carried by women. And even if male slaves carried water, they did not use pots or jugs—a domain of women—but skins (note, however, that the man is not referred to as a slave). In short, everything points to a member of the one community which did not include any women: the celibate Jerusalem Essenes. In fact, recent investigations into the chronological order of the events of Passion Week—the week leading up to Jesus' crucifixion—have resulted in an interesting hypothesis: Jesus may have used the calendar of the Essenes, fragments of which have been found among the Dead Sea Scrolls, and which was different from the other, frequently conflicting, calendars in use in ancient Palestine. Everyone had to conduct his ritual practices according to one of the current calendars, and the one used by the Essenes would be as convenient and plausible (or implausible) as any of the others.

For Jesus and his disciples, using the Essene calendar had perhaps an added advantage as it came from a group independent of the Temple and its authoritarian guardians. And Jesus may have had earlier contacts with Essenes anyway—interested as he was in the thinking and doing of all his countrymen. Essene communities existed far away from Qumran also: at and near Damascus, in the Batanaea (east of the Sea of Galilee), in Jerusalem, and elsewhere. One did not have to live at the 'monastery' of Qumran to know about Essene theology and practice.

A tangible kind of relationship between Christians and Essenes continued after the Ascension, when we find Essenes among the first converts to the faith in the risen Lord. But where, and how do we know? Read Acts 6:7: 'The number of disciples in Jerusalem increased rapidly, and a large number of priests became obedient to the faith.' What priests, you may ask. It cannot have been the Sadducees, who refused point blank to accept even the possibility of a bodily resurrection (see Matthew 22:23–32 or Acts 23:8), and it cannot have been the Pharisees, who were not led by priests. Thus, only one priestly community in Jerusalem remains— the Essenes.

Recent excavations on and near Mount Zion, the southwestern 'corner' of Jerusalem, have established that the Essene Quarter and the early Christian community were almost next to each other. What many considered to be purely legendary traditions (such as the site of the Upper Room, or the settling of the Essenes in that corner of Jerusalem—traditions passed on by Josephus regarding the Essenes and by quite a few early church historians in respect of the Christians) have been vindicated by modern archaeology. Visitors to the Protestant cemetery on Mount Zion hardly ever carry on beyond the tombs of the Bishops Gobat and Alexander or that of the archaeologist Sir Flinders Petrie. However, at the far end of the cemetery is the Essene Gate, recently rediscovered, and still so full of character, even in its fragmentary state, that it is the only one of the ancient Jerusalem city gates of which an exact elevation can be drawn. Nearby, a surprisingly large number of *mikvaot* (the purifying baths used by Orthodox Jews to this very day) have been found—two are in fact visible on the northern slope of the cemetery. In such density, they are typical of the Essenes with their extremely strict purity laws.

From the cemetery, it is not far to the *Coenaculum*, the Upper Room of the Last Supper. The Franciscan Gothic structure of the Upper Room is late medieval—wave after wave of occupiers throughout the centuries had destroyed what had stood there before. But underneath, there is the so-called Tomb of David. It is not in fact the historical tomb of King David (which was on the Ophel Hill to the east of the present Old City), but an empty crusaders' cenotaph. Behind it, however, you can still see the remaining shape of a niche, dating, like other parts of the ground floor, from the late first century AD.

In ancient synagogues, such a niche was the receptacle of the Torah scroll. But this niche is not directed towards the Temple, which it would have been in a synagogue. It is orientated straight towards Golgotha. In other words, the evidence suggests a very early Jewish Christian place of worship, retaining elements of the synagogue but relocating and redefining them in Christian terms. That niche may still have held the Torah—sacred, after all, to Jewish Christians as much as to the Orthodox Jews themselves, or it may also have contained some of the first Christian writings. Even this would have been possible, since the probable 'inauguration' of this building was not long after AD70, when Christians were allowed back to certain areas of Jerusalem after its near-total destruction by the Romans and established themselves under Simeon Bar Clopas, a cousin of Jesus. Christian inscriptions further underline the archaeological evidence.

A reliable local tradition, then—the close proximity of Christian and Essene communities, the site of the Essene Quarter, and the existence of the Upper Room above a very early Jewish-Christian church. Essenes were among the first Christian converts, Christians among those learning from the Essenes. Learning even, as some scholars have suggested, how to safeguard the strictness of their community life. The divine judgment passed on Ananias and Sapphira after their deceitful behaviour about the sharing of their possessions (Acts 5:1–11) was perhaps a direct consequence of the attempt by the early Christian community to emulate the extremely strict communal lifestyle of their Essene neighbours. If they wanted to evangelize among those living next door to them, they may have felt that they could not be less disciplined in their way of life than those they wanted to attract.

Where does all this leave us in our investigation into the writers of the first Christian texts, their materials, techniques and traditions?

The Essene Gate connects the Essene Quarter with the road leading to Jericho and Qumran. And at Qumran, near the Dead Sea, hundreds of manuscripts have been found since 1947, the well-known Dead Sea Scrolls. This term really covers other excavation sites in the area as well, such as the Wadi Murabba'at and the caves of the Bar Cochba Warriors. But for our present purposes, let us stay at Qumran, a settlement rediscovered only after the finding of the first caves with scrolls, and soon identified as the 'monastery' of the Essenes mentioned by historians such as Pliny the Elder and Josephus in the first century AD.

The Essenes at Qumran were diligent writers, copyists and collectors of manuscripts. It is, however, hard to imagine that they wrote *all* the scrolls found in the caves themselves, all the less because, with the possible exception of one disputed letter, there are no originals, only copies (some of them duplicates, perhaps, of texts despatched to communities elsewhere, and now lost). Visiting tourists are shown traces of one part of the building called the 'scriptorium' (that is, the place where the 'monks' wrote). The scriptorium itself is no longer visible—it was on the first floor—but writing utensils have been found, and empty jars; and the desks used by the scribes have been reconstructed at the Israel Museum in Jerusalem.

The Essene scribes, not unlike others of their time, preferred parchment as writing material, and the scroll as their format—the rolled-up rather than the leaf-on-leaf codex type of book. And their languages were first Hebrew, the language of the Jewish Law and of the official community literature, and second Aramaic, the language of parts of the Old Testament and the everyday language of the Essenes. The famous Isaiah Scroll, 7.34 metres long, with all sixty-six chapters of Isaiah in Hebrew, from the second century BC, is perhaps the best known Old Testament text found at Qumran. It was discovered in a jar, just as we read in Jeremiah 32:14: 'Take these documents... and put them in a clay jar so that they will last a long time.' With the exception of the book of Esther, larger and smaller fragments of all the Old Testament books have been found in those caves; and with them, some eight hundred non-biblical fragments, both in Hebrew and Aramaic.

Four *Greek* fragments in cave Four may thus be regarded as the odd exception to the rule. But what about cave Seven? There, nineteen Greek scroll fragments have been found, and not a single Hebrew or Aramaic one. All of them (except number nineteen, preserved as an impression of a fragment on petrified soil) were written on papyrus, the cheaper, more convenient material, not on parchment. Why? How can we explain the peculiarities of this exceptional cave? Could it really be that it contained Christian texts, originally written, after all, in Greek, on papyrus, and in the scroll format? This suggestion is dismissed out of hand by all those who could not possibly envisage the existence of Christian documents at a place like the Qumran of the Essenes, abandoned as early as AD68, when the soldiers of the Roman Tenth Legion destroyed it, before marching on to Jerusalem, which they took and destroyed in AD70. And yet, as we have seen, the accumulated evidence for connections between the Essenes and the first Christian community in Jerusalem would make contacts further to the south-east, via the Essene Gate, quite plausible. Indeed, looking at it from the point of view of Jesus' command to them to preach the gospel, it seems highly possible that there must have been contact.

Could the Essenes, so often—and wrongly—thought to have been the source of Jesus' own teachings, have preserved some of the first Christian documents, some of the first sources of what we know about Jesus and how we know it?

The mystery of cave Seven

One thing is certain: the scroll fragments found in cave Seven at Qumran cannot be forgeries. They were discovered in 1955. And when they were published in 1962, only two of the nineteen had been identified. They were all published, together with photographic reproductions, and as for the unidentified seventeen, possible readings for the letters on the fragments were suggested. With so many Qumran fragments waiting to be published, scholars did not see any need to spend more time on the seemingly unidentifiable ones immediately. So they were more or less left to be forgotten.

Only the first two became integral parts of studies on the Greek text of the Old Testament. They had been identified as a passage from Exodus 28:4–7 (7Q1) and from the apocryphal (that, is 'biblical' writings not accepted as being part of the canon of the Bible) book of Baruch 6:43–44 (7Q2). That was important enough in itself: to this day, only four other Greek Old Testament fragments have been found at Qumran, all of them in cave Four, all from the Torah (known in Greek as the Pentateuch—the collection of the five books of Moses), and only one of them is a papyrus fragment (the others are parchment). And what is more: the fragment from Baruch was sensational since no parts of this particular apocryphal book had been found in any of the other caves, neither in Greek nor in Hebrew or Aramaic.

So cave Seven was quite an exception. However, hardly anyone paid any attention to this unique phenomenon—a cave with nothing but Greek papyrus fragments (and the one imprint in the soil), one of them with a text unknown elsewhere at Qumran, and challengingly, with seventeen fragments still waiting to be identified. Who had collected the scrolls in this cave? Who had put them there? Who had assembled a collection at Qumran which included the unlikely combination of the Torah and an apocryphal writing?

Some years after its discovery, cave Seven collapsed and subsided into the wadi, the dried-up river bed below the settlement of Qumran. Further investigations into its structure and further finds became impossible.

Needless to say, no one had the remotest suspicion that New Testament fragments could be among the seventeen unidentified fragments from this cave. Until the likelihood of contacts between Christians and Essenes in Jerusalem and, by inference, at Qumran, had become as overwhelmingly convincing as described in the previous section, and until the assumption of dates later than AD70 for all New Testament writings except Paul's letters began to give way to a more balanced assessment of the facts, no one saw any reason to assume the existence of New Testament fragments at Qumran. It was highly unlikely that the New Testament could be left in a cave at a 'sectarian monastery' in AD68.

And yet, even before John A. T. Robinson came along in 1976 with his brilliant attempt at a re-dating of the New Testament to the period before AD70, the Spanish papyrologist José O'Callaghan suggested that at least some of the Greek papyrus fragments from cave Seven came from New Testament texts. Two of his identifications were particularly provocative: Mark 6:52–53 (7Q5) and 1 Timothy 3:16 to 4:1 and 3 (7Q4). The full text of these passages, of which only small parts have remained on the papyrus scraps, would read as follows:

'For they had not understood about the loaves; their hearts were hardened. When they had crossed over, they landed at Gennesaret and anchored there.' (Mark 6:52–53)

'Beyond all question, the mystery of godliness is great: He appeared in a body, was vindicated by the Spirit, was seen by angels, was preached among the nations, was believed on in the world, was taken up in glory. The Spirit clearly says that in later times some will abandon the faith and follow deceiving spirits and things taught by demons. (...) They forbid people to marry and order them to abstain from certain foods, which God created to be received with thanksgiving by those who believe and who know the truth.' (1 Timothy 3:16–4:1 and 3)

For Mark, this meant that the Gospel would have had to have been written some time *before* AD68—if only because the cave was closed in AD68 and the papyrus copy must have got there prior to this. For 1 Timothy, it meant that this letter—this being the first papyrus fragment of it ever found—was written so close to the lifetime of Paul that it could be, theoretically, an authentic letter of Paul's after all—contrary to the majority of scholarly opinion. And since both fragments had been dated, on the basis of their style of writing, *before* their identification to no later than AD50, the dating of the originals behind these papyri became more extraordinary still.

O'Callaghan had not even been looking for New Testament fragments at Qumran. His interest was that of the papyrologist, not the historian, archaeologist, literary critic or New Testament scholar. All he had in fact set out to do was to collect a complete and annotated list of Greek manuscripts of the Old Testament, called the Septuagint. When he came to the two identified fragments from Qumran cave Seven, his curiosity was kindled and he tried to identify at least those other fragments which were as big as the first two. All his attempts to locate any of them within the Old Testament and the Apocrypha failed. But one fragment, 7Q5, had an eye-catching combination of letters, 'nnes'. Could this, as the original editors had suggested in 1962, be part of a Greek genealogical passage? Obviously not, for none of the other letters of the fragment fitted any of the places in the Greek Bible where 'nnes' occurred.

Could it be part of the word 'Gennesaret'? In the Greek Bible, the name of the lake and the region occurs only once with this spelling, in the Apocrypha (1 Maccabees 11:67). But here again, none of the other letters of the fragment fitted. On the point of giving up, O'Callaghan tried the New Testament (he later also tried, just to make sure, several Greek authors who were known to have been read in the period concerned: without success). And in the New Testament, he found one passage which fitted all the evidence: Mark 6:52–53. Spurred on by this success, he tried to identify the other fragments and was successful with 7Q4 (1 Timothy 3:16 – 4:1 and 3).

For seven further fragments, he made suggestions for possible New Testament identifications, realizing that they were too small to be identified with sufficient certainty.

$7Q6^1$ = Mark 4:28

$7Q6^2$ = Acts 27:38

7Q7 = Mark 12:17

7Q8 = James 1:23–24

7Q9 = Romans 5:11–12

7Q10 = 2 Peter 1:15

7Q15 = Mark 6:48

They remain possibilities, no more and no less, and only on

the assumption that they *might* belong to the New Testament. They are, of course, so small that no certainty will ever be possible either way. One should not try to refute the identifications of the major fragments (as some have tried) purely because such tentative suggestions are also made.

The international reaction to O'Callaghan's identifications was mixed: some, particularly in the English-speaking countries, and Italy and Spain, hailed them as breakthroughs, an opportunity to challenge 'liberal' theology. But such extreme assessments only hardened the opposition from other schools of thought. Opponents from all parts of the theological spectrum, again often from the English-speaking world, but mainly from Germany, refuted the identifications as impossible, as fantasy.

Some time in the late seventies, the debate petered out, and scholars no longer dared to mention these Qumran fragments, for fear of rejection by the scholarly community. Only recently, I was criticized myself, in a review of a book to which I had contributed, for taking these fragments seriously. But this is precisely the point: the questions raised at the beginning of this chapter had never been answered. Most of the criticism levelled at O'Callaghan's identifications was unfounded—the debate had to be re-opened.

I had the privilege of being able to work with the original papyri, not merely with photographic reproductions, on three separate visits to the John Rockefeller Museum in Jerusalem where they are held. And I realized, initially to my own surprise, that even the toughest questions about difficult readings, uncommon features and textual peculiarities could be answered from within the context of first- and second-century papyrology and textual tradition. I found further paleographical details—that is, concerning the handwriting—and I had to admit that the evidence for the correct identification of the major fragment, 7Q5—Mark 6:52–53—was overwhelmingly strong. Later I added 7Q4—1 Timothy 3:16 – 4:3—to this 'list' and regarded, as

O'Callaghan did, the others as 'possible' with varying degrees of probability.

It would need a whole book in its own right to describe the fragment in detail and to analyze all the pros and cons fairly. That is why I have written articles which were followed by such a book which now exists in German, Dutch, Italian and Spanish versions and of which an up-to-date, entirely rewritten English version, *The earliest gospel manuscript?*, is being published by Paternoster Press.

It is enough to say here that not only is the fragment of Mark identifiable by certain tell-tale characteristics, also confirms its great age precisely because of a couple of exceptions to the text of all other, later, manuscripts of this Gospel. There is the omission of the words 'epi ten gen' (to the land) before 'Gennesaret' in line 3 (Mark 6:53). Readings of other early versions of this story in the Gospels do not include these words either—words which were surplus to requirements before AD70, when the 'gen', the inhabited land of Gennesaret, still existed. Only after AD70, in other words, after the date of this fragment, when the settlement was destroyed by the Romans, would there have been any necessity to add these words to differentiate between lake and land. Before AD70, they would have been superfluous.

Similarly, our oldest fragment of John's Gospel, the p52, does not include the repetition—found in all later fragments—of the 'for this' in chapter 18 verse 37. Could it be that the very first authors and scribes did not like the rhetorical flourish of such superfluous words which later readers and copyists, working, as we know, for a mainly listening public, added for effect?

The other peculiarity of this Greek fragment is this: in line 3, the word 'diaperasantes', which means, loosely translated, 'having crossed over', begins with a *t* instead of a *d* as in 'correct' Greek. Is this an argument against identification? Far from it. It is the very exception to the rule which we might expect in a very early, pre-AD70 papyrus connected with eyewitness accounts from Palestine, particularly from

Jerusalem. For if we compare it with the famous 'Temple barrier' stone, often shown in illustrated books on biblical archaeology, a stone which would have been in full view of every visitor to the Temple, it has exactly this variant of spelling of *t* for *d* in the word 'tryphakton' (or rather 'dryphakton') which means barrier. So was there an alternative pronunciation and spelling in Jerusalem and the surrounding area? Why not? And the one man credited with being the most likely author of Mark's Gospel, the Mark whose mother owned one of the houses where the first Christians met (Acts 12:12), came from Jerusalem.

There is a conclusive number of arguments, discussed in Part I, that Mark's Gospel was written in Rome. And in Qumran cave Seven, a jar was found with an inscription in Hebrew letters, 'rwm'', which would sound like 'Roma' or 'Ruma'. One of the great Qumran scholars, Joseph Fitzmyer, has suggested that this could have been a way of writing 'Rome' in Hebrew letters, and this Hebrew spelling is indeed documented elsewhere with the meaning 'Rome'. There are examples of jars, from Gibeon and Succoth, where an inscription denotes not the name of the owner of the jar but its place of origin. Whoever put the fragments (or some of them) into this jar before they were put away and closed up in cave Seven—a Christian visitor, a Qumran or Jerusalem Essene, whoever it was who wanted to safeguard them from destruction by the approaching Romans—he will have used this opportunity to mark the jar with the place name of the origin of its contents. Even if the scrolls had come to Qumran from Jerusalem, at least the Jerusalem Christians would have known that they were of Roman origin. Such a valuable gift originating from the community in the very heart, the capital of the Roman Empire, cannot have been forgotten or neglected.

Assuming a Christian origin, even the seemingly incongruous combination of the Torah and an apocryphal fragment in cave Seven would make sense: the first Christians held the Torah and indeed the whole Old

Testament (which was, after all, their Bible before the New Testament grew as a collection) in the highest possible esteem. To have the Torah represented by the Exodus fragment, along with a Gospel scroll, represented here by Mark, would be the perfect combination. And even the Apocrypha, books not included in the canonical Hebrew Old Testament, were so popular among Jews and Jewish Christians that their knowledge—and usage—is actually presupposed in some New Testament writings.

As late as about AD200, the popularity of apocryphal stories was still a matter of debate among Christians. There is a famous letter from Julius Africanus to Origen, in which Julius demonstrates conclusively that the story of Susanna cannot be an authentic part of the canonical Hebrew book of Daniel, and must therefore be regarded as apocryphal. And Julius Africanus applies techniques of analysis in which modern textual critics could take pride.

Some of the unidentified 7Q fragments remaining (especially the more substantial 7Q3 and 7Q19) could eventually prove to be remnants of unknown contemporary Jewish/Jewish Christian writings, texts as lost as, say, the *Assumption of Moses*, or the *Apocalypse of Elijah*. Then there are the unknown texts from which the quotations in Matthew 2:23, John 7:38, Ephesians 5:14, 2 Timothy 3:8 and James 4:5 are taken, or known but lost writings such as the true first letter to the Corinthians (see 1 Corinthians 5:9), and the letter to the Laodiceans (Colossians 4:16).

The Christians left Jerusalem at the beginning of the Jewish uprising against the Romans, in AD66. The historian Eusebius tells us that they left for Pella, a place in Transjordan. AD66 is thus the most probable, or at least the latest possible, date for the transfer of the scrolls from Jerusalem to Qumran. And we are faced with fragmentary traces of what are indeed the oldest remnants of the textual tradition of the New Testament, old enough still to bear the hallmarks of the people who wrote the original texts themselves.

PART III

HOW JESUS CAME TO ROME

In the world of the first Christians, Rome was the centre of the world and the Roman Empire the greatest influence upon their lives. In Part III we look at how Christianity came to Rome, and how the existence of the Roman Empire influenced its spread.

The wealth of archaeological evidence, both in Jesus' own Nazareth and Capernaum, and in Rome is stunning. And we look at the questions: did the people mentioned in Paul's letters really exist? Are the traditions passed on about Christianity true? How many 'relics' are genuine? Did Jesus Christ visit Rome?

7
Rome—Centre of the World

In this chapter we look at how Christianity came to Rome and also look at one of the riddles presented by one early historian: was Jesus Christ in Rome?

Rome was the centre of the world in which the first Christians lived. Antioch, Alexandria, Athens all had their own claim to fame, either past or present, real or imagined, and they all played their part in the history of the early church. But Rome was the capital of the Empire, the political centre, the melting-pot of nations and peoples. In New Testament times, up to sixty thousand Jews lived in Rome—almost as many people as lived in the whole of Jerusalem, for which estimates vary between fifty and ninety-five thousand.

How the message came to Rome

Jews and converts to Judaism from Rome were among the very first to hear the gospel of the risen Christ when Peter gave his great 'sermon' in Jerusalem on the day of Pentecost (Acts 2:10). As visitors to Palestine, they would have returned to Rome and so were potentially the first messengers of the new faith to the city, as early as AD30, twelve years before Peter's first stay, and some twenty-nine years before Paul's.

We do not know how many of them were actually Roman citizens. The privilege of Roman citizenship was either a

107

birthright, as it was for Paul, or could be bought for considerable amounts of money, or granted as a right accompanying the setting free of slaves.

There is an incident in the New Testament, involving Paul, which illustrates this: 'As they stretched him out to flog him, Paul said to the centurion standing there, "Is it legal for you to flog a Roman citizen who has not even been found guilty?" When the centurion heard this, he went to the commander and reported it. "What are you going to do?" he asked. "This man is a Roman citizen." The commander went to Paul and asked, "Tell me, are you a Roman citizen?" "Yes, I am," he answered. Then the commander said, "I had to pay a big price for my citizenship." "But I was born a citizen," Paul replied.' (Acts 22:25–28).

The name of this commander is given as Claudius Lysias (Acts 23:26), the Gentile name 'Claudius' indicating the acquisition of citizenship during the rule of Claudius (AD41–54). The historian Cassius Dio complained, in his *Roman History*, that the wife of Claudius, the notorious Messalina, profited from an efficient form of bribery which had been built into the system of applications for citizenship. Paul, however, was born a Roman citizen, which means that at least his father, if not earlier ancestors, must have been granted this important privilege back in the city of Tarsus. In any event, the commander Claudius Lysias was impressed by Paul's superior type of citizenship, and his attitude towards the apostle all at once becomes almost over-protective. To guard him from an imminent assassination attempt, he sends him to Caesarea with an escort of no less than two hundred soldiers, seventy horsemen and two hundred spearmen (Acts 23:23).

As for the Jews in Rome, we may assume that a considerable number of them possessed Roman citizenship. When Jews were expelled from Rome by Tiberius in AD19, some four thousand men who were Roman citizens, and would therefore have had to be sentenced individually, were not expelled but drafted into a kind of auxiliary army to fight bands of robbers in Sardinia. To these four thousand, add their families, and the estimated number of Jews with Roman citizenship is ten or twelve thousand in Rome alone.

The expulsion of Jews and Jewish Christians by Claudius in AD49, mentioned in several Roman sources and in Acts 18:2, only affected those who were not Roman citizens. And however many of the first Christians were Roman citizens, Aquila and Priscilla, Paul's valuable friends and supporters, were apparently not among them. They were, after all, expelled from Rome straightaway.

But what evidence do we find of Romans and Roman citizens in the new Testament? There are quite a few examples.

Roman citizens have dealings with Jesus—the centurion at Capernaum (Matthew 8:5–13), the commander of the Roman detachment arresting Jesus (John 18:12), Pontius Pilate, the centurion at the cross (Mark 15:39), and, perhaps, the soldier who pierced Jesus' side with a spear (John 19:34).

Roman citizens witness and share in later New Testament events—the 'visitors from Rome' in Acts 2:10; the centurion Cornelius in Acts 10:1–48; the proconsul Gallio in Acts 18:12–17; the centurion and the commander Claudius Lysias in Acts 22:23 – 23:30; the governor Felix and his wife Drusilla in Acts 24:1–27; his successor Porcius Festus in Acts 24:27 – 26:32; the centurion Julius in Acts 27:1–43; the chief officer Publius and his father in Acts 28:7–8; the anonymous soldier(s) guarding Paul constantly and thus witnessing all his teaching for two whole years in Acts 28:16–31; the palace guard of Philippians 1:13; Theophilus, the dedicatee of Luke's writings (Luke 1:3, Acts 1:1); and, of course, Paul himself (Acts 16:37–38, 22:25–29, 23:27).

At least one other New Testament Christian was a Roman citizen: Silas/Silvanus, the trusted companion and assistant of Paul and Peter. His citizenship is mentioned in Acts 16:37–38. And quite a few of Paul's companions and the addressees of his letters may have been people with Roman citizenship:

see, for example, the 'lists' of friends he mentions in Colossians 4:7–17, Romans 16:1–24, 2 Timothy 4:9–21. Philemon himself was a Roman, as were others mentioned in Paul's brief letter to him.

So the world of Rome was not alien to the followers of Jesus, the apostles and their companions, even before the first of them actually set foot in the city. Indeed it would have been so familiar to them that it is almost surprising that it took them so long to get there. Peter, as we saw in Part I, waited until AD42. And Paul went 'compulsorily', in around AD59, although he had frequently expressed his desire to go there before. 'After I have been [in Jerusalem],' he says in Acts 19:21, 'I must visit Rome also.' In his letter to the Romans, which was written in Corinth, to people he had never met, he states that he is 'so eager to preach the gospel also to you who are in Rome.' In fact, Jesus himself tells him to go: 'Take courage,' the Lord says to him in a night-time vision, 'as you have testified about me in Jerusalem, so you must also testify in Rome.' (Acts 23:11).

Nevertheless, Rome and the Western world took second place in the list of priority mission fields, coming after Jerusalem, Judea, Samaria, Galilee and other areas of the eastern provinces. It was the logical sequence, after all. And furthermore, Rome was not regarded as the ultimate target: Paul intended to continue further to the west, to Spain (Romans 15:24–28), and some scholars think that he managed to do so during the years which are not recorded after the end of the book of Acts. There are sources which suggest Paul did visit Spain. Clement of Rome, in his first letter, usually dated around AD96, but probably written as early as AD70, says Paul 'reached the limits of the west'. And there are other, later, sources for this. Indeed, neither Peter nor Paul, when they finally *did* travel to Rome, went entirely voluntarily. Had they had the choice, they might have waited even longer.

In the meantime, Christianity had already spread to Rome without them. One might say that Peter was at least indirectly responsible for this, as a result of preaching that Pentecost sermon in Jerusalem. A hint of such early beginnings may be seen in Paul's letter to the Romans, chapter 15, verses 20–22. 'It has always been my ambition,' Paul writes, 'to preach the gospel where Christ was not known, so that I would not be building on someone else's foundation... This is why I have often been hindered from coming to you.' Many scholars in this century have seen in this statement a reference to Peter. His name, of course, did not need to be mentioned: the Romans at that time knew who Paul meant.

It looks as though Paul's hesitancy—eventually overcome by Jesus' own command in Acts, chapter 23, and by the Romans putting him on a ship to Rome as a prisoner—was based on an agreement between the apostles not to infringe on each other's founding authority. In 1 Corinthians 3:10, Paul looks at the procedure from the other side: 'By the grace God has given me, I laid a foundation as an expert builder, and someone else is building on it.' And again Paul does not mention names although the Corinthians must have known to whom he was referring.

But whoever the 'someone' who had laid the foundations may have been, a Christian community existed in Rome for a considerable time before Paul's visit. His postscript to his letter to the Romans presupposes the existence of several well-established house-churches. There is the house-church of Aquila and Priscilla (who had returned to Rome after the edict of their expulsion had lapsed with the death of Claudius in AD54). There is the house-church of Aristobulus, as well as the one run by Narcissus, and we may assume also that Andronicus and Junias led a house-church. And then there are the two lists of people who practically make up house-churches in their own right—'Asyncritus, Phlegon, Hermes, Patrobas, Hermas, and the brothers with them', and 'Philologus, Julia, Nereus and his sister and Olympas and all the saints with them'.

By AD59, Roman Christian delegations were confident enough to go out to meet the prisoner Paul and his Roman guards, outside the city, on the Via Appia, at Forum Appii and Tres Tabernae, as described in Acts 28:15.

Anyway, no one can deny the presence of Christians in Rome by AD49 at the latest. Otherwise, it would have been difficult for the Emperor to expel them from the city in that year! Furthermore, the highly-respected Roman historian Suetonius appears to claim that somehow Christ himself had appeared in Rome and had caused the tumult which led to this expulsion. *Christ in Rome?* Did Suetonius know something Luke, Paul and Peter did not?

Was Christ in Rome?

The clue that unlocks this strange statement of Suetonius, that Christ was in Rome, is to be found on the Via Appia, that marvel of Roman engineering, which Paul would have travelled to reach Rome.

'The queen of long distance roads,' the Roman author Statius called it. Begun in 312BC, and finished in 191BC, the Via Appia ran between Rome and Brundisium (modern Brindisi), the port which linked Rome with Greece and the Eastern Mediterranean. The route, 375 kilometres, 234 miles long, went via the coastal resort of Terracina, wealthy Capua in the Campagna, and the legendary port of Tarentum.

In New Testament times, travellers from Sicily would (like Paul in Acts, chapter 28) have joined the Via Appia at Forum Appii. On their way, they would have journeyed through Rhegium along the Via Popilia. Or, if they preferred to go by the sea route from Rhegium, faster than travelling along the road given good weather conditions, they would have disembarked at Puteoli (modern Pozzuoli), like Paul and his companions. This passage in Acts (28:11–16) describes in some detail Paul's journey to Rome, and the Christians, 'brothers', who met them, first those at Puteoli, and later the Roman Christians who came out to meet them at the Three Taverns near Rome.

Puteoli was Rome's most important port for trade with

112

Egypt and the Levant. Seneca, the Roman historian, writes in a letter, dated around AD63, about his stay in the port of Puteoli: 'Unexpectedly, ships from Alexandria arrived today... the so-called sea mail ships; they announce the following grain fleet. A welcome sight for the Campagna! The whole population stands on the jetty of Puteoli and recognizes, in the swarm of ships, those of the Alexandrians by their rigging.' Puteoli was one of those places where not only mail and grain were unloaded, but also the latest news, together with the people who brought it.

Pagan cults had established themselves in Puteoli long before they had become commonplace in Rome, a Jewish community is documented there, pre-dating the one in Rome, and those first Jewish hearers of Peter's Pentecost sermon in Jerusalem must have stopped at Puteoli on their way home. And indeed, there was apparently a hospitable Christian community in Puteoli when Paul arrived there in AD59: 'There we found some brothers,' Luke writes in Acts 28:14, 'who invited us to spend a week with them.' And we may gather from Luke's account that even Paul's Roman guards enjoyed their stay with these Christians: otherwise they would have made their prisoner leave the place immediately.

Having left Puteoli, Paul, like other travellers, would have continued his journey by ship along the coast up to Terracina, where the canal called Decemnovium began. It crossed the Pomptine marshes, plagued with malaria and infested by bands of robbers. Travellers would disembark from their canal ships at the Forum of Appius, to continue by road along the Via Appia. The Forum of Appius was a convenient meeting place and thus the one chosen by some of Paul's Roman Christian friends. From there, it was a mere sixty-two kilometres to Rome.

People used the Forum of Appius to rest before continuing to Rome, which was a good day's journey away. One of the letters of Cicero, the controversial politician and philosopher, mentions the next stopover on the way, Tres

Tabernae ('Three Taverns'), some forty-eight kilometres south-east of Rome, where another group of Roman Christians met Paul. Nothing of this place remains, apart from a few walls and buried traces on private property, not yet accessible to archaeologists.

Here, the road was magnificent, uninterruptedly straight, continuing for some forty kilometres: a model of the archetypal straight Roman road. It was an engineering triumph which must have inspired the admiration of many a traveller.

Nearer Rome, that stretch begins which is usually visited by modern tourists: lined by tombstones, some of them imposing, others destroyed or left to slow decay. There, opposite the Casa Rotondo, the alert traveller finds a small stone with an odd inscription. It mentions several names, and one of them is *Chrestus*. A few kilometres further on, next to the tomb of Caecilia Metella, there is another such inscription, again mentioning a certain *Chrestus*, a *lictor* ('attendant') of the Caesar. These are two of many occurrences of this particular name—a name derived from the Greek for 'good', 'kind', 'sweet', and frequently used. But what does it mean? In short, it is the clue to the riddle behind Suetonius' statement which seems to imply that Christ was in Rome.

Why should Suetonius say Christ was in Rome? One of the first things to realize is that, at the time of the first Christians, certain Latin and Greek vowels were pronounced alike. Thus a long *e* and *i* would sound exactly the same. 'Christos', Greek for Christ, sounded like 'Chrestos', and Latin Christus (for Christ) sounded like Chrestus, too. So there would have been a confusion of sounds.

What then does Suetonius actually say? In his biography of Emperor Claudius, he writes: 'He expelled the Jews from Rome, who were constantly causing tumults on the instigation of Chrestus.' We are back in AD49, the year when Claudius expelled all Jews (and Jewish Christians) from Rome, recorded in Acts 18:2. And what Luke does not

114

say in so many words, Suetonius explains: Christ had been behind the public unrest among the Jewish community of Rome, a situation which had prompted Claudius to expel the ringleaders and their followers—with the exception of those who possessed Roman citizenship.

Apparently, the active missionary work of the Jewish Christians among their fellow Jews had so enraged the latter that near-riots had broke out, infringing public order. This sort of thing had happened before: in Acts, starting in chapter 6, we read about such an incident in Jerusalem leading to the death of Stephen. Then again in Acts 13:49–50, public unrest was caused in Pisidian Antioch, so that Paul and Barnabas were expelled from that region.

Or read this about Corinth: 'While Gallio was proconsul of Achaia, the Jews made a united attack on Paul and brought him into court. "This man," they charged. "is persuading the people to worship God in ways contrary to the law." Just as Paul was about to speak, Gallio said to the Jews, "If you Jews were making a complaint about some misdemeanour or serious crime, it would be reasonable for me to listen to you. But since it involves questions about words and names and your own law—settle the matter yourselves. I will not be judge of such things." So he had them ejected from the court. Then they all turned on Sosthenes the synagogue ruler and beat him in front of the court. But Gallio showed no concern whatever.' (Acts 18:12–17)

Gallio, a brother of the philosopher and letter-writer Seneca, was less rigorous than Claudius, and perhaps he was right: the effect of his action—or rather inaction—was that Paul could 'stay on in Corinth for some time' (Acts 18:18). In Rome, however, Claudius had to deal with a community of some sixty thousand Roman Jews—a mass riot among them (and this was possible as far as he was concerned) had to be prevented, and expulsion was a well-tried means of achieving this end.

Suetonius, writing much later in his biography of Claudius, clearly thinks that 'Christ' was behind the riot:

the grammar of his sentence tells us that he was thinking of a particular individual actually present in Rome. Suetonius wrote around AD120, some seventy years after these events. His sources will have mentioned that name. Suetonius, who was not particularly interested in Christianity and who had no means of distinguishing between the title 'Christus' and the proper name 'Chrestus', did the obvious thing: he took 'Chrestus' to be just one of many bearers of that name, inscriptions of which are still to be found along the Via Appia today. What he was not able to appreciate at the time was the accuracy of his mistake, and the information which actually lay behind the source he used: Chrestus, that is Christ, was indeed in Rome, but in a different sense. The Jewish Christians were taking the message of the risen Lord to their fellow Jews. And thus, it was indeed 'on the instigation of Christ' that the gospel was preached. And it was this 'gospel' which was the cause of the riots, both at Rome and elsewhere.

Some interpreters of this passage in Suetonius' *Life of Claudius* have suggested that the Roman historian was thinking of some obscure Jew called Chrestus, a man who was some kind of political activator, inciting mob unrest. But 'Chrestus' is not documented as a Jewish name. And could a non-Jew really have caused Jewish riots? It is true that Suetonius called the Christians 'Christians' with an *i*, in his *Life of Nero*, but for someone who does not quite know how to interpret his sources, this does not amount to much. Anyway it is quite usual for authors and scribes to use variant spellings for the same words in ancient texts. Tacitus, writing some fifteen years before Suetonius, calls the Christians 'Chrestians', confirming the plausibility of Suetonius' 'mistake': 'To get rid of the rumour [of his responsibility for the fire]', Tacitus writes, 'Nero substituted as culprits others on whom he inflicted the most exquisite punishments. These people, hated for their disgraceful activities, were called Chrestians by the populace. This originator of this

116

name, Chri*s*tus, had been executed during the reign of Tiberius by order of the procurator Pontius Pilate.'

The Christian author Tertullian, writing at the end of the second century, enjoys the possibilities of this uncertainty in spelling, and he plays on the variant spellings and meanings. '"Christian", as far as it can be translated, comes from "anointed",' Tertullian tells his non-Christian readers. 'But when you wrongly render it as "Chrestian" (for you do not even know what the name as such means), it is composed from sweetness or kindness. Thus, in innocent men even the innocent name is hated.'

Tertullian, a master of the art of how to turn the tables, pinpoints one of the sadder aspects of early Christian (and some of modern Christian) history: Christians were hated, persecuted and often martyred, and their message caused public riots, even when all they were offering was a message of kindness, of neighbourly love—the message of the Christ who was in Rome, not only in AD49.

Paul's letter-box

'Because sleep is lacking, many sick people perish here in Rome. And their sickness comes from poor digestion and the heavy, stomach-inflaming food. But who can sleep in those rented flats? It costs a lot of money to sleep in the city, and that's where the rot sets in. Night after night, coaches roll around the narrow corners of the streets, where whole herds block the traffic and the curses of the drovers fill the air. It is a noise to wake up even an inveterate sleeper like Claudius! The crowd moving in front of me hinders my hurried step and behind me the masses are pressing on. One pushes an arm into my side, another a hard piece of wood. Now a beam hits me on my head, then a barrel of oil. Filth sprays my calves, from all sides I get kicked by heavy soles, and a soldier drives the nails of his boots into my toes.

117

'Think of other dangers threatening us at night: from those sky-scraping roofs, tiles often fall and crash down onto our heads. And the windows: how often does someone throw old and broken crockery down into the street, with such force that the surface of the road is damaged with holes. If you do not make your will before you go out for an evening meal, people will think you are lethargic and indifferent to a sudden fate. For as many open and yawning windows there are on your route, as many ways there are to a sudden death! Now you have an idea as to why I am leaving Rome.'

These excerpts, freely translated, are not from the letter of a fed-up Roman in the 1990s, but by Juvenal, the great satiric poet, from his third satire published in around AD100. And Juvenal does not skip the street gangs, the bands of thieves and muggers flooding the city from the Pomptine marshes, unpleasant encounters at every corner. The scenes he depicts are an accurate portrayal of Roman life both before and after the great fire of AD64. The fact that Juvenal mentions Claudius, the emperor who ruled from AD41 to 54 and who was renowned for his sound and imperturbable sleep, highlights the unchanging, chaotic unpleasantness of life in Rome under the emperors. It seems that Nero was not all that unhappy about the fire of 64: it gave him a chance to remodel the city, with wider streets, better houses, and more open spaces. But less than forty years later, under the emperor Trajan, when Juvenal wrote his satires, things were just as bad as they had been before the fire.

Yes, Rome was truly the 'Babylon' Peter calls it at the end of his first letter and which John, the author of Revelation, condemns in words as biting and bitter as anything Juvenal or his fellow satirist, Persius, ever wrote:

'The merchants of the earth will weep and mourn over her because no one buys their cargoes any more—cargoes of gold, silver, precious stones and pearls; fine linen, purple, silk and scarlet cloth, every sort of citron wood, and articles of every kind made of ivory, costly wood, bronze, iron and marble, cargoes of cinnamon and spices, of incense, myrrh and frankincense, of wine and olive oil, of fine flour and wheat; cattle and sheep; horses and carriages; and bodies and souls of men.

'They will say, "The fruit you longed for is gone from you. All your riches and splendour have vanished, never to be recovered." The merchants who sold these things and gained their wealth from her will stand far off, terrified at her torment. They will weep and mourn and cry out,

"Woe! Woe, O great city,
dressed in fine linen, purple and scarlet,
and glittering with gold, precious stones and pearls!
In one hour such great wealth has been brought to ruin!"

'Every sea captain, and all who travel by ship, the sailors and all who earn their living from the sea, will stand far off. When they see the smoke of her burning, they will exclaim, "Was there ever a city like this great city?"' (Revelation 18:11–18)

Somewhere amid this turmoil, in the reality of Rome— satirically and prophetically described in all its unpleasantness, the first Roman Christians lived and passed on the gospel message. The names of these first Roman Christians abound—even if, for obscure reasons, some scholars maintain that all these names are legendary. For these were real people, living in the real world. Legends may indeed have distorted the telling of the lives of some of the real early heroes. After all, who has not heard 'legendary' stories about such popular figures as Churchill, Montgomery, Kennedy and other famous people in history? But does anyone—simply because such legends *do* exist—doubt that the people concerned did?

Peter and Mark were in Rome, Paul and Luke were in Rome, Silas/Silvanus, Aquila and Priscilla were in Rome—

these are sober New Testament facts. Obviously, all the other Christians Paul sends his greetings to at the end of his letter to the Romans were in Rome too. And if Paul was in Rome by the time he wrote his second letter to Timothy (as has been once again convincingly argued in a recent stimulating study by Michael Prior, and in a commentary by Gordon D. Fee), the people mentioned at the end of the letter, sending their greetings with Paul's to Timothy, were in Rome too: Eubulus, Pudens, Linus, Claudia and others.

Paul, as we know, was under house arrest in Rome, but he was allowed to live in a rented house, to receive visitors, and to teach. The people who visited him there and heard him must have had names. Why should the names linked with these men and women be, by tradition, the invention of later legend-writers? Historians should not accept such dismissive judgments. But there are *some* 'historical' traditions which make truly entertaining stories.

When I was in Rome again recently, I visited the place said to have been the house of Paul. You cannot miss it: outside, the sign is 'still' there: *Sancti Pauli Apostoli Ospitium et Schola*, 'Hospice and school of St Paul the Apostle', it says, in Latin. The site is now occupied by the church of San Paolo alla Regola, not far from the river Tiber, in an area where the first Christians did indeed live. And underneath the church, excavations have yielded impressive parts of several first-century houses. Did Paul stay there after all?

At the time of my recent visit, the excavated underground area was flooded—still a frequent occurrence in Rome, particularly at places close to the river. I spoke to one of the Franciscan monks who guard the church and live in a monastery next door. 'Well,' he said, 'maybe Paul forgot to turn his bath water off when he left for Spain.' Did he believe that, behind his anecdote, there was a real Paul staying at the house found underneath this church? He smiled wisely. One cannot prove it either way. Paul could have been there, of course. No other place in Rome claims that it was the site of his rented house. But the tradition is late, and the letter-box with his name on it has not been found.

We can laugh at the idea of Paul's letter-box, of course. But we should never forget—and it cannot be stated often enough—that these were real people in real times and living under real conditions.

The Christians in Rome were in touch with their 'brothers and sisters'—other Christians—all over the Empire: they needed the contact and exchange, eager as they were to learn from each other's experiences, and as normal human beings they made the most of the available means of communication to do so. Postal services did exist, and they were quite efficient. Paul, Peter and others not only wrote letters, but also received them. Sometimes these would have been carried by couriers or travelling missionaries: there are references to, for example, taking and delivering a letter, and to the work of Tychicus and Onesimus, mentioned in Colossians 4:7–9.

In other cases, the imperial postal services may have been used. This was a privilege normally only granted to civil servants and the military. Theophilus might have used them for the distribution of copies of Luke's Gospel or Acts. Ordinary citizens would have paid so-called *tabellarii*, letter-carrying messengers, to do the task. Pliny the Younger, that energetic letter-writer who corresponded with his emperor, Trajan, about appropriate interrogation techniques for Christians in AD112, used the imperial post when he wrote to the emperor; but for his private correspondence he employed freelance *tabellarii*: 'I have fulfilled my promise,' he writes to his friend Arrianus, 'and have done what I promised in my previous letter—you will have received it, as I gather from the time past, since I gave it to a fast and diligent *tabellarius*. Unless, of course, something happened to him on the way.'

These messengers were paid twice, both by the sender and by the addressee—a system still profitably used by parcel post in Germany, for example. And they could be very fast indeed. If the conditions were favourable (depending on the winds, season, and so on), it would have taken a ship five days to link Corinth in Greece and Puteoli in Italy. This is no modern estimate, but information drawn from the period: a feat not often repeated today, given the present condition of Greek and Italian postal services. It is recorded that the Roman military leader Cato once managed to reach Africa from Rome in under three days. But there were other extremes too, under less favourable conditions. It once took Cicero two months to get to Rome from Ephesus, in October/November—a delay much more familiar to modern postal service users.

Exchanging news, despatching long letters of exhortation (like the letter to the Romans or the first letter to the Corinthians): this was nothing out of the ordinary. It was normal, it was an everyday experience. When the seven churches of Asia (Ephesus, Smyrna, Pergamum, Thyatira, Sardis, Philadelphia and Laodicea) received the letters sent by John and quoted in Revelation 2:1 – 3:22, they would not have been surprised that they *received* the letters, but they may have been at their content.

We are dealing with realities here; and, simply put, the consequences are staggering: the author of Revelation could have been informed about the decadent way of life in Rome by eyewitness account within a week or a fortnight.

Peter and Mark in the early forties, Paul, Peter, Luke and Mark in the early sixties, they all knew what it meant to live in Rome and they would not have kept silent about their experiences. They are sure to have passed on even more information than we are here given in the documents which have survived.

When Peter returned to Jerusalem after his first stay in Rome, AD48 at the latest (the probable date of the Jerusalem Council described in Acts 15:4–30), he would not have kept quiet about city life under Claudius or about Claudius' allegedly promiscuous wife Messalina. Nor would Mark when he joined Barnabas and Paul on their first missionary journey (Acts 13:1–5).

Scholars sometimes maintain that it took a very long time for news, concepts, documents and so on to reach people and to influence individuals and communities. This is plainly not borne out by the facts. Why talk in terms of years or decades, if all it needed was a good ship, appropriate weather conditions and a fast messenger to get news about life in Rome to places such as Jerusalem or Patmos, where the book of Revelation was written, in less than a month? Why doubt the existence of one or even several copies of Mark's Gospel in a cave at Qumran before AD68, if less than a month was needed for a courier to reach Jerusalem from Rome?

Strangely enough, people tend to think that communication and development of ideas among the Christian communities of the first century was an extremely slow, cumbersome process. Frequently, fifteen years or more are estimated for the time it took Matthew or Luke to come up with their versions of Mark's Gospel once they or their communities had received their copies from Rome. Would not a month, or let us say three, be much more realistic? Are we really compelled to believe that it took the Colossians a period of umpteen years rather than a couple of weeks or months to read Paul's letter and to pass it on to the Laodiceans and to read that written to the church at Laodicea as he charges them to do? (Colossians 4:16) Was Matthew (or Luke for that matter) so slow and stupid that it took him a decade or two before he finally digested Mark's Gospel and managed to hold a pen in his trembling hand again?

Too many of our modern reconstructions are based on a poor understanding of the period, on present-day wishful thinking, or exaggerated scepticism, rather than on the available facts about New Testament times.

8
A Wealth of Archaeological Evidence

The site of Paul's rented house may never be established with absolute certainty. But there are quite a few traces of authentic first-century Christian houses, three of them at least linked with Jesus himself. One of them we have already looked at in Part II: the Upper Room of the Last Supper, in the house later turned into the first Jewish-Christian 'synagogue' we know of. Interesting traces of first-century Jewish, and, later, Jewish-Christian houses, have been found at the two places connected with earlier parts of the life of Jesus, before he began his work as a wandering preacher: Nazareth, where Jesus was brought up, and Capernaum.

Nazareth and Capernaum

At Nazareth, tourists immediately head for the modern Church of the Annunciation: a building so modern, big and ugly that anything authentic inside or underneath it is difficult to imagine. And yet, underneath the area covered by the present structure, storage caves and living areas have been excavated which do at least demonstrate beautifully and impressively what the first-century home of Jesus might have looked like.

There is one cave which typifies the large multi-purpose 'house' of that time: to the front, on the left-hand side, the animals would have been kept—marks of the hooks in the wall

124

where some of them were tethered can still be seen. At the back, in the middle of the cave-like structure, the family, sometimes three generations together, would have lived. The two areas were divided only by a low step. And to the right, the 'kitchen', where the oven was, can still be seen, the remains of black soot still on the wall. This one-room, stable-cum-living quarters concept had many advantages: one of them was the use of the animals as a source of warmth in the winter. Although central heating had already been invented by the Romans at that time, it was not available to ordinary people.

Nearby, an early second-century Jewish-Christian baptistry has been found, and remains of a third-century church with graffiti—writing on the wall—dedicated to Mary. Another graffito shows John the Baptist, holding a long staff with a cross in his right hand. Similar early traces have been discovered under St Joseph's Church next door, which, according to tradition, is on the site where Jesus grew up. An early Jewish-Christian baptistry and a habitable cave are all that have been found, and since the tradition itself is much later than these finds (sixteenth century), it may be doubted if they are really related to Joseph, Mary and Jesus.

The most fascinating discoveries, however, have been made underneath the monastery of the 'Dames of Nazareth', which has fortunately been spared, as yet, the onslaught of mass tourism. Here, an undoubtedly first-century house has been found, which was later incorporated into a Byzantine building, and, later still, into a Crusaders' church. Archaeologists and historians are beginning to think that this, rather than the area underneath St Joseph's Church, is the authentic site of the house of Joseph, where Jesus grew up, and that it is the place alluded to by early fourth-, fifth- and sixth-century pilgrims. Early local traditions can be very faithful and reliable; here, tradition and archaeology seem to converge.

Not far from the first-century house, a tomb with a round stone to block its entrance was recently discovered, in perfect condition—the stone can still be rolled into place. Both Matthew and Mark give explicit descriptions of Jesus' tomb (see Matthew 27:60 and 28:2, and Mark 15:46 and 16:3–4). Compared with extant tombs in Jerusalem, this one in Nazareth much more closely resembles the type of first-century tomb we are led to expect by New Testament accounts about Jesus' burial and resurrection.

These archaeological remains underneath the monastery of the 'Dames of Nazareth' preserve not only the extant traces of the kind of house Jesus would have grown up in, but also the type of tomb he was to be buried in many years later in Jerusalem. One is somehow reminded of the tradition in certain parts of Europe where an empty coffin is kept in the house, tailor-made for the oldest member of the family. It reminds us of the Latin words Martin Luther used for one of his most impressive hymns: *Media vita in morte sumus*, translated in the Book of Common Prayer as 'In the midst of life we are in death.'

As we have seen, the traditions behind sites where there are authentic archaeological finds need not be entirely unreliable, but having said as much, it is easy to be taken in. The so-called Pilgrim of Piacenza, an anonymous author, writing around AD570, tells his readers that he saw the synagogue of Nazareth, and in it a leaf on which the Jesus-child had written the letters of the alphabet. This story is followed by an anecdote about a wooden beam kept at the synagogue, on which Jesus and his playmates sat. Christians could move and lift it, but Jews could not make it move in any way at all. The synagogue has been re-excavated, but the leaf and the beam have gone. Good news for all those who do not cherish dubious relics.

There are plenty of dubious relics around. For some people, they hold a morbid fascination. At the church of Santa Croce in Gerusalemme in Rome—in a side chapel built when Mussolini was in power (and the architecture reflects this unmistakably)—a gory collection is on view to the credulous public. There is the horizontal beam from the cross of the 'good thief' (see Luke 23:40–43). The man was called Dismas—at least this is what the description says, adopting the embellishments of later legend and improving, of course, on the much too sober Gospel accounts... Up another flight or two of stairs there is a collection which includes thorns from Jesus' 'crown' (Mark 15:17), the sign fastened to the cross, with the Hebrew, Greek and Latin inscription (John 19:19–20), one of the nails of the crucifixion, and a piece of wood from the cross, and, especially ghoulish, the finger with which Thomas touched the wounds of Jesus. (John 20:27–28)

But what about the seamless robe of Jesus for which the soldiers cast lots (John 19:23–24)? After all, it is famous thanks to that awe-inspiring Hollywood 'great', *The Robe*, starring Richard Burton. Unfortunately for the custodians at Santa Croce in Gerusalemme, this is kept at the Cathedral of Trier in Germany. An irreverent anecdote relates how a visiting priest at once pointed out to his colleague in Trier that this robe could not be authentic because of the designer label saying 'Made in Hong Kong'. Years later, the two meet again, and the priest from Trier proclaims triumphantly, 'It must be authentic after all. I have found an invitation to the wedding at Cana in one of the pockets!'

Rome, however, still heads the league table for relics, for within its walls there is also the staircase which Jesus is said to have climbed at the praetorium of Pontius Pilate: the so-called *Scala Santa*. Helena, Emperor Constantine's mother, found it in Jerusalem, which was quite an extraordinary feat since archaeologists have only recently established the actual position of Pilate's praetorium—not at the Antonia Fortress or at Herod's Citadel, as commonly thought, but at the Hasmonean Palace.

But it is easy to mock all this. It has often been alleged, for example, that the splinters of the cross preserved and revered world-wide would yield a whole forest. However, the French author Ernest Hello calculated in 1858 that even twice the number of pieces would only amount to one tenth of the whole cross.

The whole question of relics is often overshadowed by legendary stories and fantastic creations. But belief in the value of items linked with heroes of the faith existed even in New Testament times. 'And everywhere he went—into villages, towns, or countryside—they placed the sick in market places. They begged him to let them touch even the edges of his cloak, and all who touched him were healed.' (Mark 6:56) Or again, we read in Acts 19:12, of Paul: 'Handkerchiefs and aprons that had touched him were taken to the sick and their illnesses were cured and evil spirits left them.'

Much damage has been done both by the 'relic merchants' and by the gullibility of those who venerate such relics. So scepticism is called for whenever claims are made. More often than not, it can be established that such 'relics' are not authentic, but serious scientific and historical analysis is always required.

Recently, the 1988 carbon-14 dating of the Turin Shroud proved, or so it seemed, that the shroud was a medieval artefact produced roughly between 1260 and 1390. However, it has been demonstrated by scholars from the United States of America and Germany that these tests were manipulated. For example, the pieces of the shroud to be tested were taken from an area that had been severely damaged by fire and water in the Middle Ages and exposed to medieval handling when people tried to save and protect it. In other words, a medieval carbon-14 date was a foregone conclusion with such examples! The tests will probably be repeated, under strict and neutral supervision. But this scandal (and a scandal it is no matter what one may think about the Turin Shroud itself) has not strengthened the position of those who are sceptics on principle, lacking in openness of mind and fairness of method.

The results of the excavations at Nazareth, some of which have not even been published yet, are less well-known than those at Capernaum, the setting for so many scenes in the Gospels. Peter had a house there. And in Capernaum, we are on very firm ground indeed. As early as 1916, an octagonal building was discovered south of the ancient synagogue. Archaeological analysis has established that this is a fifth-century church, built upon earlier structures going right back to the first half of the first century.

It soon became obvious that the oldest structure was a first-century house and that the later buildings on top of it were memorial sites and churches. Fish hooks, lamps (see Acts 20:8), graffiti with the names of Jesus and Peter, and other Christian artefacts have been found. There could only be one house in Capernaum worthy of such continuing interest and veneration from the first century onwards—the house where Jesus stayed; the house of Peter. Fourth-, fifth- and sixth-century pilgrims mention it; the earliest extant account by the Spanish pilgrim Etheria in around AD390 calls it a house-church. That is, a house turned into a church, with the original walls still standing.

Jesus had moved to Capernaum before the calling of the first disciples (Matthew 4:13–22), and it became his home: 'Jesus stepped into a boat, crossed over and came to his own town,' it says in Matthew 9:1. However, Capernaum, like Nazareth, was to refuse to repent, and Jesus would later condemn it: 'And you, Capernaum, will you be lifted up to the skies? No, you will go down to the depths. If the miracles that were performed in you had been performed in Sodom, it would have remained to this day. But I tell you that it will be more bearable for Sodom on the day of judgment than for you.' (Matthew 11:23–24). Here the two pairs of brothers, Peter and Andrew, and James and John, had their fishing boats. Here Peter's house became the assembly point for people eager to listen to Jesus, and this was where he stayed.

'As soon as they left the synagogue,' writes Mark about Jesus and the people at the synagogue, 'they went with James and John to the house of Simon and Andrew.' (Mark 1:29). And from the following account, it is obvious that Jesus stayed there: 'Simon's mother-in-law was in bed with a fever, and they told Jesus about her. So he went to her, took her hand and helped her up. The fever left her and she began to wait on them. That evening after sunset the people brought to Jesus all the sick and demon-possessed. The whole town gathered at the door, and Jesus healed many who had various diseases.' (Mark 1:30–34).

It follows that the authentic house of Peter must have had a kind of square or 'plaza' in front of the entrance. And indeed, right in front of the only entrance of the original building, facing east, there is a street and such a square.

Another incident helps us to visualize Peter's house: the healing of the paralysed man. 'The people heard that he had come home. So many gathered that there was no room left,' Mark writes in chapter 2, verses 2–5, 'not even outside the door, and he preached the word to them. Some men came, bringing him a paralytic, carried by four of them. Since they could not get him to Jesus because of the crowd, they made an opening in the roof above Jesus and, digging through it, lowered the mat the paralysed man was lying on. When Jesus saw their faith, he said to the paralytic, "Son, your sins are forgiven."'

Archaeological reconstructions have established that the walls of the houses in Capernaum were about three metres high and were covered with a roof made of reed and cane work, insulated and sealed with loam. We can actually picture those four men 'digging through' the roof: the classic example of an accurate eyewitness account—Peter's, on whose preaching Mark's Gospel is based.

Until 1988, the remains of Peter's house and of other houses nearby could still be seen, in relation to the synagogue opposite. But no longer, for under the pretext of protecting it, the Franciscan custodians of the site have erected an enormous, and extremely hideous, concrete structure above it. Peter's house has become a museum piece, pretending to be a twentieth-century church. Ancient

Capernaum, as originally discovered by archaeologists, is spoiled for ever.

It is small comfort that a few years ago the exact site of the first-century synagogue was established, the synagogue attended by Jesus, Peter and the others. But the building now on view is late fourth century. Underneath, a third-century synagogue was traced. And underneath that, under the central aisles of the fourth- and third-century buildings, the floor of the first-century synagogue was discovered. The floor alone measures some eight by twenty metres, and some scholars think that the beautiful carved stone with the seven-branched candlestick (the menorah), and the ram's horn (the shofar) found during excavations belonged to this synagogue.

In any case, this first-century synagogue is linked with another person living at Capernaum: the Roman centurion mentioned in Luke 7:1–10. This man had built the synagogue, which probably means that he gave considerable amounts of money to the local community for this comparatively large building (it was approximately four times as big as the synagogue at Magdala, for example). Luke even provides the reason: 'Because he loves our nation,' the Jews tell Jesus. Jesus heals the centurion's servant, and in Luke's account the house of the centurion is mentioned and the fact that he was still in active military service: 'I myself am a man under authority,' he says to Jesus, 'with soldiers under me. I tell this one "Go", and he goes; and that one, "come", and he comes. I say to my servant, "Do this", and he does it.'

Therefore it had been puzzling that no trace of a Roman garrison or barracks had been found nearby. Some sceptics went so far as to doubt the historical authenticity of the episode because of this lack of archaeological evidence. In 1986, however, the archaeologist Vasillios Tzaferis established the existence of a first-century building complex, including typical Roman baths. This would have been the site of the centurion's garrison. It can be seen in the

131

area of Capernaum which belongs to a Greek-Orthodox community, separated from the Franciscan part by a stretch of land (and a wall) which was apparently also uninhabited in New Testament times: this would tie in with the description of Jesus' walk to the house of the centurion, which reads as though the house was some distance from the densely populated area of Capernaum proper.

So the Capernaum of Jesus and Peter, with the house where they lived and worked, and where Jesus taught and healed, has come to life again. We can visualize it as a major fishing town, a busy port, with a customs area big enough to deal with sea trade as well as land trade between the two tetrarchies of Philip and Herod, and with a Roman garrison guarding the district. Industry (glassware, oil presses, grain mills) and agriculture (oil, grain) flourished at Capernaum, in addition to the profitable fishing business serving the whole country as far as Jerusalem and beyond.

The Greek geographer Strabon (64BC – AD19) provides an illuminating piece of information: in his *Geography*, he writes that 'the fish from the Sea of Tarichea [Tarichea was Greek for Magdala, and so refers to the Sea of Galilee], which is prepared and salted in local factories, makes for a delicious meal [in Rome].' Dried and pickled fish from the area of Capernaum appeared on Roman dining tables in New Testament times and before—historically documented, and an interesting glimpse of the importance of the international trade which was a part of the daily lives of Peter and the others. One might even entertain the amusing thought that Peter, when in Rome, had fish for his meal which had been caught and pickled by some of his former partners or employees.

Meeting places in Rome

Now, let us go back to Rome and find the first traces of Christian sites there. What can be said about the place where Peter taught, where Mark wrote his Gospel, and where that

Gospel was rolled up and sealed for despatch to Jerusalem? Where did the Christians live, celebrate communion, or baptize, in New Testament times?

The life of the early church followed the example given by Jesus: when he did not preach and teach in the open air, he chose private houses for his gatherings, be it Peter's house in Capernaum or the Upper Room in the Essene house in Jerusalem. The synagogues also were often used for 'lectures', as we see in Luke, chapter 4. And several times Paul and his companions preached the gospel in synagogues: at Damascus (Acts 9:19–20), Salamis (Acts 13:5), Pisidian Antioch (Acts 13:14–43), Iconium (Acts 14:1). It is interesting to note this last reference: 'At Iconium, Paul and Barnabas went *as usual* into the Jewish synagogue.' Then there were the synagogues in Thessalonica (Acts 17:1–4), Berea (Acts 17:10), Athens (Acts 17:16–17), Corinth (Acts 18:1–4), Ephesus (Acts 18:19; 19:8), and at Jerusalem (Acts 24:12).

These synagogues were by no means the purpose-built establishments we see today. Quite frequently, they were parts of residential buildings, or a storey of a private house. A well-known example of this from pre-New Testament times was found at Delos (dated to the first century BC). Other, later examples can be seen at Stobi (Yugoslavia), Dura Europos (Syria), Priene (Turkey), Aegina (Greece) and Hamman Lif (Tunisia), to name but a few: in fact they were scattered all over the Roman Empire. The first-century Jewish-Christian synagogue church in Jerusalem is another case in point: it was established at the house of the Last Supper, not long after AD70, some forty years after the event it later helped to commemorate took place.

So it is hardly surprising that Christians did not build proper churches when they began to establish themselves in the cities of the Empire. They would not have had the necessary funds in most cases, and they were, in those pre-Constantine days before AD312, an endangered minority religion, despised if not actively persecuted by the authorities and by their religious 'rivals' alike. Public, ostentatious activities such as building a church would have been quite inadvisable. Anyway, they were happy to follow the example set by Jesus and assemble in private houses, provided by wealthier friends and benefactors. This brought two additional advantages: it saved them from investing in permanent structures (upkeep and other overheads), and also the few things really needed for a communion service could be hidden quickly and without much fuss in case of a house search by persecuting authorities.

The one famous early exception confirms this rule. It is the cross found in Herculaneum—the town destroyed in the eruption at Pompeii. The cross was probably permanently fixed to the wall until someone removed it before destruction. A box of dice found in a cupboard underneath suggests that the Christian occupants had to leave the room at some stage and took the cross with them; only the marks remained. This, at any rate, is suggested by the unmistakable traces left on the wall.

Sceptics have tried to explain it away, claiming that Christians did not use the cross as a symbol until the fourth century, but recent archaeological and historical analysis has demonstrated its authenticity as a Christian cross. Since Herculaneum was destroyed with Pompeii and other places with the eruption of Vesuvius in AD79, the cross must have an even earlier date than this. It may have been attached to the wall in the 'quiet' period after the persecution under Nero (AD64–68). The next serious persecution began only after the destruction of Herculaneum, in about AD95, when Domitian had several leading Christians executed or banished. In any case, the room of the cross was not a separate building: it was again the 'upper room', on the top floor of a private house, and therefore not easily accessible to unwelcome fellow citizens and informers.

From what we know of the historical evidence, any Christian might easily have had a cross in his house. Jesus spoke of his cross, and used it as a symbol, and Paul presented it as one in his letters. A statement such as Mark 8:34 would have been reason enough for a Christian to put a cross on the wall of his room: 'Then he called the crowd to him along with his disciples and said: "If anyone would come after me, he must deny himself and take up his cross and follow me."'

One passage in Paul's letter to the Galatians may have been understood in the sense of the cross being not only a metaphorical, but also a visible symbol: 'Those who want to make a good impression outwardly are trying to compel you to be circumcised,' Paul writes in Galatians 6:12. 'The only reason why they do this is to avoid being persecuted for the cross of Christ.' Or read Philippians 3:18: 'For, as I have often told you before and now say again even with tears, many live as the enemies of the cross of Christ.' There are many other such references to the importance and meaning of the cross, both in the Gospels and in Paul's letters. In intellectual Roman circles, however, the cross was the symbol of a poor, outcast criminal—a man executed as an enemy of the state.

The New Testament historian Leslie W. Barnard recently explained that scholars who doubt the significance of the Herculaneum cross have been victims of their own logic. They claim that because finds of Christian crosses in any number can only be dated to the late second century, and even then only in the form of anchors, tridents or ships, then a pre-AD79 cross is a pure anachronism—something out of its real, historical context. Real crosses, they say, appear in significant numbers only after the conversion of Emperor Constantine. And so it can be deduced that a cross found in the first century cannot be Christian at all. Perhaps it is unfortunate for theoreticians that Herculaneum with its cross was quite accidentally preserved, thanks to the eruption of Vesuvius. Without it, even this solitary witness might not have survived and those who maintain that Christians began to make use of the cross only later would not have to try to explain it away.

Another pre-AD79 cross was found at Pompeii, in a house on the insula XIII, in the first region of the town. It even has an inscription in initials (VIVV) which may mean (but nothing depends on this) Vivat (crux) vivat—the cross may live, it may live. Barnard suggests that the first Christians were quite free to use the cross in the first century, in their private homes. Only when they actively engaged in public philosophical and theological debate did they regard it as unwise to refer to the cross—a symbol to the Romans of the execution of an enemy of the state. The first Christians used symbols familiar to their pagan observers which could easily be given Christian meaning: the Good Shepherd, the philosopher, the praying man or woman with outstretched arms, or the victorious hero. In fact the only very early depiction of Christ's passion is in a Roman catacomb, in the Catacomb of Praetextatus, late second- or early third-century. This shows Christ wearing laurel leaves, surrounded by people with palm branches, the symbols of victory.

By the time Minucius Felix, a Roman lawyer of African origin, wrote his *Octavius*, around AD166, pagan citizens knew that the Christians had crosses as objects in their homes. Two characters in the work mention this: and one of them explains that they are not used as objects of idolatry. He then goes on to enumerate pagan and everyday examples of cross-like symbols. Indeed, the occasion and circumstances when references to the cross were made were chosen very carefully. This was not to ignore its role in Christian tradition, of course, but rather to stress other facets of Christianity, those not entirely foreign or potentially offensive to the pagan enquirer.

And just as the first-century Christians felt comfortable in using the symbol of the cross within their own four walls, second- and third-century Christians felt equally at ease not using it obtrusively. Paul himself, in his one classic speech to philosophers—fellow 'intellectuals' if you like—on the Areopagus in Athens, did not mention it (Acts 17:22–31). Jesus had briefed his followers on the appropriate tactics: 'I am sending you out like sheep among wolves. Therefore be as shrewd as snakes and as innocent as doves.' (Matthew 10:16)

Minucius Felix provides an interesting testimony to the lack of overtly Christian buildings in Rome at the time he was writing. He was the first Christian to write a published (and extant) work in Latin. Many scholars still think that Minucius should be dated to the early third century, after Tertullian, the great Christian thinker and theologian. But it can be shown, both on the grounds of textual and other evidence, that the *Octavius* was probably written as early as AD166 (the date given above), during the reign of Emperor Marcus Aurelius. It was a period punctuated by sporadic and cruel persecutions in the provinces (most notably the public slaughtering of men, women and children at the theatre of Lyons in AD178), but Christians moved freely in Rome itself.

In *Octavius*, a dialogue, Minucius introduces us to three old friends (one of them is Minucius himself) who meet again after a long time. They walk along the beach at Ostia, and one of them reveals that he is not a Christian by bowing to a statue of the god Serapis. The discussion switches to religious questions. They decide to hold a kind of debating contest, with Minucius acting as referee: Caecilius Natalis, the non-Christian, advocates the pagan position, and Octavius Januarius, the Christian, follows with the Christian reply. The contest ends with defeat being conceded by Caecilius, and the three of them continue their stroll along the beach, knowing that 'some minor difficulties', which they will take up on the following day, remain outstanding. They walk on into the sunset, 'cheerful and light-hearted'.

This is not the place to do justice to this gem of an early piece of Christian apologetic writing. But what is of interest here is one passage in the anti-Christian speech by Caecilius Natalis: 'Why such efforts to hide and keep secret the object of their veneration, when honourable things always enjoy publicity, while evil things are secret? Why do they [the Christians] have no altars, no temples, no known idols, why

137

do they never speak publicly, why do they never meet openly, if it is not for the reason that what they venerate and conceal is punishable and shameful?' The Christians, he says, are 'a cowardly and shady lot who keep silent in public but are garrulous in the corners'.

In his reply, Octavius Januarius not only refutes the accusation. He also highlights a theological aspect of Christian reticence: 'Do you think that we conceal what we venerate because we have no shrines and altars? What image of God should I devise, since, if you think about it seriously, man himself is the image of God? What temple could I build for him, since the whole universe, the work of his hands, cannot contain him? ... But, so you say, we can neither show nor see the God whom we venerate. But this is precisely why we believe in this God, because we can feel him even if we cannot see him.'

This dialogue was written by a Christian who presents the antichristian position from his own daily experience. In this work there are also several quotations from an otherwise lost antichristian writing by the rhetorician Fronto, and they, too, demonstrate the attitude of the pagan majority—that Christians were not 'obtrusive' in public, but people felt their growing presence: in them they sensed an uncertain threat to their own beliefs, and since no 'hard facts' were available, rumours abounded and led to hostility out of which came persecution.

Octavius lists a number of accusations made against Christians—among them infanticide, the worship of an ass, sexual perversions, blood drinking and cannibalism. It was a 'no win' situation, but, even so, the Christians preferred to stay in private homes. The building of churches, even if possible financially, would have been tantamount to inviting trouble. Minucius Felix does inform us, though, about the existence of separate rooms in private houses, set aside for meetings and worship. In Caecilius Natalis' antichristian diatribe, we find the following sentence; 'And since evil always spreads luxuriantly... the abominable places of worship (*sacraria*—chapels, rooms where something holy is venerated) of this despicable and impious lot multiply.'

This is the first explicit reference to such separate Christian assembly rooms. But there are earlier traces, beginning with the New Testament itself. For example, after his escape from the prison of Herod Agrippa II, Peter goes to the house of Mary, the mother of Mark, 'where many people had gathered and were praying' (Acts 12:12). In other words, it was a known meeting place. But even Peter could not just walk in; he had to pass a kind of security check before he could be admitted to the actual room, and, in this case, there is an amusing misunderstanding (one of several instances, incidentally, where the New Testament does betray a sense of finely-tuned humour). 'Peter knocked at the outer entrance, and a servant girl named Rhoda came to answer the door. When she recognized Peter's voice, she was so overjoyed that she ran back without opening it and exclaimed, "Peter is at the door!" "You're out of your mind," they told her. When she kept insisting that it was so, they said, "It must be his angel." But Peter kept on knocking, and when they opened the door and saw him, they were astonished.' (Acts 12:13–16)

A tradition which can be neither proved nor rejected, given the present state of archaeological and historical investigation, was that this house belonging to Mary, Mark's mother, was on the site where the Syrian Church of St Mark in the old town of Jerusalem now stands. It has a more secure place in the annals of biblical studies for a quite different reason: it was here that the first Dead Sea Scrolls were brought in 1947 and kept before their publication. If you go there, you will see that the structure of the church still reflects the description of the house in Acts. Whatever the legitimacy of its claims, it has the same aura of the period, as, say, the one which the definitely inauthentic 'Garden Tomb' preserves—unlike the historical site in the Church of the Holy Sepulchre.

For those who have the rare privilege of making the

personal acquaintance of one of the monks of St Mark's, another early Christian element may come alive again. My wife and I once had supper with the monk who works there as manuscript illuminator and, before we sat down to eat, he recited the Lord's Prayer in Aramaic, the native language of Jesus and of these Syriac Christian monks. Give or take a few minor changes in linguistic features over the centuries, we heard it in the very form in which Jesus himself, and later his first followers in Jerusalem—and perhaps on the very spot—had said it.

New Testament references to Christians assembling for worship in private homes are quite frequent. For example, see 1 Corinthians 16:19: 'Aquila and Priscilla greet you warmly in the Lord, and so does the church that meets at their house.' Also, we read Paul's greetings at the beginning of his letter to Philemon: 'To Philemon, our dear friend and fellow-worker, to Apphia, our sister, to Archippus our fellow soldier and to the church that meets in your home.' Two more examples appear in Paul's letter to the Romans, the first again referring to Aquila and Priscilla: 'Greet Priscilla and Aquila, my fellow workers in Christ Jesus... Greet also the church that meets at their house.' (Romans 16:3 and 5). And in Romans 16:23: 'Gaius, whose hospitality I and the whole church here enjoy, sends you his greetings.' There are yet more references—Colossians 4:15 and Acts 16:40.

Jesus himself set a precedent by choosing to meet with his disciples in an upper room. It seems that his followers also preferred meeting upstairs. Peter's house in Capernaum had only one floor, but the Last Supper was held in 'a large upper room, furnished and ready'. When the Jerusalem Christians met again after the ascension of Jesus, 'they went upstairs to the room where they were staying' (Acts 1:13). And at Troas, 'there were many lamps in the upstairs room where we were meeting' (Acts 20:8). The Troas report is even more precise than that: in spite of the many oil lamps, or perhaps because of the fumes emanating from them, and in view of the late hour (Paul 'kept on talking until midnight'), a young man named

Eutychus, seated near a window, fell asleep and 'fell to the ground from the third storey'. This may have been the top floor of the building.

Houses with more than two floors were the exception: the *domus*, the house of Roman aristocrats, high-ranking officers, or senators—the detached villas—hardly ever exceeded two floors. But the blocks of rented flats, known as *insulae*, mostly inhabited by several tenants, always consisted of many stories. In Rome, four to six were the norm, and the record was held by the *insula* of the *Felicula*, a first-century tenement house described by Roman authors as something of an abnormal skyscraper. It must have exceeded the limit set by Nero (20.65 metres), already an increase on the legal maximum of 17.70 under Augustus. Even in those times, there were ways and means of evading the legal limits. But the Felicula building must have been exceptionally tall. Tertullian, the Christian author of the late second and early third centuries, describes the absurdity of the Valentinian sect by likening their theology to the Felicula block of flats. There, 'under the highest roofing tiles, they place God'. It is a system, Tertullian writes, 'which rises to the sky with as many storeys as the block of the Felicula in Rome'.

The largest blocks of flats would have housed up to three hundred people, but less than one hundred would have been the rule. In any case, the *insulae* provided anonymity. This would have been a welcome protection for Christians; but an unwelcome source of loneliness and isolation for many tenants, in just the way that modern high-rise flats are today. Christians would have chosen the top floors also for strategic reasons: no one could 'happen' to pass an upper floor room, and so the danger of being detected was much reduced.

Visitors to Rome can see one impressive ruin of a multi-storey block or *insula*: the early second-century building just to the left of the stairs leading up to the church of Santa Maria in Aracoeli on the Capitol Hill. It had at least five storeys, and a ground floor with shops. There are other buildings with three visible storeys at the Market of Trajan, a house underneath the church of St Anastasia, where two storeys can still be seen, and the remains of a house can be visited underneath the church of Santi Giovanni e Paolo, also with two storeys still standing. Of most of the other extant houses—and we shall look at those in a moment—only the ground floor has been preserved or is reconstructable. But, however extensive the remains may be elsewhere, no 'upper' or 'top floor' as referred to in the New Testament has remained intact. And so, with the one exception of the upper floor room with the cross at Herculaneum, preserved by the lava, ashes and mud from the eruption of Vesuvius, the lack of concrete archaeological evidence for first-century Christian assembly rooms is obvious: where there is no chance of finding anything, nothing can be found.

This, however, is not the end of the quest. For there are other avenues to be explored.

9

Jerusalem in Rome

There can be no doubt that the Christians in Rome must have lived somewhere. Even Paul lived at a rented house and this cannot be disputed simply because we have not found that letter-box with his name on it. One way of spotting the likely places at which Christians must have lived is by studying a combination of New Testament allusions, later literary sources from Rome, and archaeological data.

The oldest Roman churches

Four New Testament people are linked with existing Roman churches built on top of first-century houses. First, there are Aquila and Priscilla. They are linked with the church of Santa Prisca on the Aventine Hill. New Testament evidence is unequivocal: they were leaders of a house-church community in Rome (Paul writes: 'Greet also the church that meets at their house,' Romans 16:5). This couple was affluent, apparently with branches of a tent-making business in Rome, Corinth (Acts 18:1–3) and Ephesus (Acts 18:26). Paul, at one stage, was employed by them (Acts 18:3). They were obviously financially secure enough to have been able to own a house in a prestigious area like the Roman Aventine.

Some scholars have suggested that Prisca/Priscilla, normally named first, before her husband, by Paul, was a member of the noble Roman family of the *gens Prisca*. In this case, she might have converted to Judaism when she married

Aquila (both are described as Jewish Christians by Luke in Acts 18:2) and would have left Rome with him, after Claudius' expulsion of Jews and Christians in AD49, out of loyalty to her husband. If she was indeed of noble origin, even greater access to wealth and prestigious addresses might have been possible. But, as tent-making traders on an international scale, they would have been rich enough anyhow.

At Corinth, a private house from the time of Paul has been excavated. The dining-room alone (and, as we already know, this was a favourite Christian meeting place in the early days), measured more than forty square metres. The Villa of Anaploga, as it is called, represents the type of house people like Priscilla and Aquila may have owned. Or perhaps it belonged to a man like Gaius, who, according to Romans 16:23, accommodated Paul and 'the whole church' of Corinth at his house.

In Rome, traces of a spacious first-century house were found underneath the church of Santa Prisca. By the middle of the third century at the latest (the period of the devastating persecutions of Decius), a shrine of the popular god Mithras was installed there, the remains of which can still be seen today. But either before or after this persecution, in any case before Constantine's acceptance of Christianity, the church of Santa Prisca had acquired a certain importance. Adolf von Harnack, not exactly a conservative scholar, suggested that this could have been the administrative seat of the Roman church in the third century.

The second Roman church associated with a New Testament person is San Clemente, at the foot of the Caelian Hill and not far from the Colosseum (finished under Titus in AD80). This church is traditionally regarded as having been built over the house of Clement, who was, according to Origen's early third-century commentary on the Gospel of John, and later sources, the man who sends greetings with Paul in Philippians 4:3, later becoming a successor of Peter as overseer or 'bishop' of the Roman communities. He may also be identical with the author of the apocryphal First Epistle of Clement to the Corinthians. Jerome, the fourth-century church historian and Bible translator, confirms this link; and the official sixth-century records of the Roman church underline Clement's connection with the residential area at the Caelian Hill.

Archaeological evidence suggests that there was at least one house underneath the church of San Clemente which existed before the fire of AD64, and that a new and more spacious house was built out of the ruins soon after the fire. Further first-century traces have only recently been found, during the installation of a ventilation system underneath the present-day church. Just next door to the first-century house, in a neighbouring *insula* or block of flats, a shrine and a school dedicated to the god Mithras, beautifully preserved, were established during the second century or later. This would have been during the period when Christians were forced to leave their homes and house-churches, but perhaps it is simply an example of Christians, Jews and pagans living as close neighbours. Some graveyards and catacombs even demonstrate this proximity. Among the tombs of San Sebastiano in Catacumbas, there is one, known as the tomb of Hermas, which was shared by a family with some Christian and some non-Christian members. There are many more examples to be found as far north as Trier in Germany, all dating from before the time of Constantine.

But could a mere Christian, or even a 'bishop', afford to live in such a house? It is possible, if we take seriously an early tradition which claims that this Clement was a member of the family or household of the Roman consul Titus Flavius Clemens, a cousin of Emperor Domitian. Domitian had designated the two sons of this Clement to become his heirs. But when it became known that Clement was an active Christian, Domitian had him executed for atheism (in the eyes of Roman law) and indifference to the interest of the state in AD95. He sent Clement's widow Flavia Domitilla into exile on the island of Pandateria.

Domitian behaved differently towards Christians when he sensed no political or social danger. The second-century Christian author Hegesippus relates how two grandsons of Judas, the brother of the Lord, were interrogated by Domitian. He had been told that they belonged to the royal line of David. Would they be potential trouble-makers? When it became clear that they were comparatively poor labourers and that the Kingdom of Christ was 'heavenly and angelic', he despised them as simpletons, released them and stopped the persecution of the church. This, in any case, is how Eusebius, writing in the early fourth century, quotes from the otherwise lost account of Hegesippus' *Church History*.

However, Domitilla's administrator, a man called Stephanus, led a group of conspirators against Domitian and assassinated him on 18 September AD96. Nerva, the new emperor, recalled Domitilla from exile and restored the family's property to her. Thus, soon after AD96, the family and household could have been back at the house now underneath San Clemente.

The Domitilla Catacombs at the Via Ardeatina, of a slightly later date, are situated on family property. Inscriptions on tombs can be seen which include names of members of the Flavian family.

Even if this Clement was not a member of the family or household of Titus Flavius Clemens nor his wife Flavia Domitilla, the fact remains that there was a high-ranking Roman civil servant—a consul—and his wife who were Christians at the time of Domitian. Their house, wherever it was, would have been the gathering place for a house-church almost by definition, given the New Testament and early Christian precedents.

The third Roman church connected with a New Testament person is Santa Pudenziana, at the ancient Vicus Patricius (the modern Via Urbana). The way in which the name is now formulated is misleading: it is not the church of someone called Pudenziana, but the church 'of Pudens', grammatically rendered 'Pudenziana'. Pudens has always been regarded by tradition as the man of that name in 2 Timothy 4:21: 'Eubulus greets you, and so do Pudens, Linus, Claudia and all the brothers.'

'Pudens' is a nickname, not a family name. Nicknames could be inherited, but it will always be difficult to say for certain whether people with the same name are relatives. In any case, the name Pudens appears more than once in New Testament times—on a funerary urn of the mid-first century at the Land Museum of Trier, with the name of Lucius Magius Pudens, and also on a first-century tombstone. The poet Martial refers to his friend Aulus Pudens in several of his poems, and other names from the list in 2 Timothy 4:21 appear in his epigrams. But attempts to demonstrate that Martial's Pudens, Linus and Claudia are identical with those of 2 Timothy have failed.

The earliest surviving documents dealing with the Pudens of 2 Timothy 4:21 call him a senator and equate him with the owner of a house at the Vicus Patricius. Here, it is said, Peter lived during his second stay in Rome, after AD59, and here he baptized Pudens. Later, with Paul, he also baptized Pudens' daughters, Potentiana and Praxedis.

These documents, registers of the Roman church and early 'travel guides' hardly reach beyond the sixth century and one may be inclined to mistrust them for this comparatively late date alone. However, excavations under the present church have yielded an extensive house, built probably in the Republican period (before 27BC) and in the first half of the first century at the latest. Unfortunately, tourists cannot visit it as the water table in this area is so high that it is flooded most of the time. On my first visit, I was advised to come fully equipped with diver's gear, including an underwater torch—there was no electricity of course.

The archaeological evidence strengthens the traditional claim that there was a first-century senatorial house underneath the later church. Nothing more—but also nothing less—can be said.

According to one source, the *Acts of Potentiana and Praxedis*, Pudens himself turned his house into a kind of parish church, a building given over entirely to the Christian community for their purposes. Parts of this area were turned into public baths in the second century. It remains an open question whether this was a harmless development which simply made the most of the ready availability of water there, or if it was yet another example of Christian property being taken away from its owners in times of persecution, as was probably the case under Santa Prisca and San Clemente. Parts of these baths can still be seen from outside, in the Via Balbo.

The churches of Santa Pudenziana, Santa Prisca and San Clemente were all completed in the fourth century at the latest, after Constantine, and they all belong to the group known as *tituli*—that is, churches with the 'title' of a person who at some previous stage owned the property later turned into the church. There are at least two other first-century buildings which became *tituli* churches in Rome: Santa Anastasia at the Palatine, and San Lorenzo in Lucina at the Campus Martius, the Mars Field. The latter is still being excavated. This church was even used for the election of a pope, Damasus, in 366. But its Christian roots lie in an *insula* and a house found underneath, which may well go back to the second half of the first century.

At the church of San Lorenzo, there is one vantage point in the excavation area where past and present come together as in no other Roman building. Standing in a first-century area, one looks up through a metal grille in the ceiling of the crypt, which is, at the same time, a grille in the floor of the church above. The church itself is a medieval basilica-type building with baroque artwork visible on the ceiling above. As a visitor walks through the church above, the journey from the first, via the fourth and sixteenth centuries, to the twentieth is complete.

Nearby, but still belonging to the same complex, a *pozzo*, or well, has been found which some archaeologists regard as part of a shrine of the goddess Lucina (another name of Juno). If it were a pagan site, that would assist them in their interpretation of the name of the church—not the name of a Christian woman, but of a pagan cult. On the other hand, church archaeologists have suggested that this 'well' is an early baptistry—if so, it would be one of the oldest, if not the oldest, ever found. Having seen it myself recently, I opt for a third alternative. It looks like a first- or second-century water tank with several distributing channels, a type known from Nîmes in France and other places. At an *insula*, a multi-storey apartment block, it would have been a practical installation. Perhaps the further excavation of this area will reveal more.

As this conflict of views illustrates, it is hardly ever possible to reach a unanimous opinion and draw conclusions in first-century archaeology. Unless a discovery is totally unambiguous, questions will remain unanswered and opinions will differ. For our purposes, though, it is helpful to note that archaeological evidence does appear to support early Christian traditions which have been handed down to us.

Other places remain to be properly analyzed and evaluated in the future, most notably the rooms underneath the church of Santa Maria in via Lata. There is more down there than just the fifth-century Christian 'soup kitchen' found long ago, and it would be entertaining, to say the least, to find out more about the origins of the local tradition which links this site with a stay by Peter, Luke and Paul.

But even more recent than the excavations underneath San Lorenzo in Lucina are those still going on underneath the renaissance Palazzo della Cancellaria. Here, under the courtyard, the church of Pope Damasus has been brought to light and identified (the same Damasus who was elected at San Lorenzo in Lucina in AD366). Under this church, remains of houses going back to New Testament times have been discovered. Was the church built on the private property of Damasus' family, a pagan/Christian family with very early Christian connections? It is probably so.

But let us return to Santa Pudenziana. For here the faithfully preserved local tradition and the valued origins of the site culminated in an extraordinary feat of early Christian art. Pope Siricius (AD384–399) crowned the church built by his predecessor Damasus with the earliest and most glorious apse mosaic in Rome and indeed of Christendom. It was finished under Pope Innocent I (402–417), and even though it was severely damaged by eighth- and sixteenth-century building work and 'redecoration', its early splendour is still revealed.

The first impression is of the bearded figure of Christ, sitting on a throne in the centre. Behind, there is the hill of Golgotha with a giant cross. To the left of Golgotha, fourth-century Jerusalem is depicted: the cupola of the Resurrection Chapel built by Constantine on the left, and the Church of the Ascension on the Mount of Olives on the right. So the traditional sites of crucifixion, resurrection and ascension are portrayed here just as they were shortly after the time of Constantine.

Above these buildings, the four symbols of the evangelists—lion, ox, man, eagle—taken from visions of Ezekiel (Ezekiel 1:5–10) and Revelation (Revelation 4:6–8) have been incorporated. The 'face like a man' is on the left, the eagle on the right, but these two have been partly destroyed by reconstruction work done in the late sixteenth century. To the left of the cross is the winged lion, to the right, the winged bull. Ten apostles are visible standing on both sides of Christ enthroned, five to the left and five to the right. The two closest to Christ are singled out—each accompanied by a young woman holding a laurel wreath over his head. Portrayed thus, they are meant to be Paul (left) and Peter (right) with the women Potentiana and Praxedis behind them.

The whole conception of the mosaic is multi-faceted, and a hidden meaning is equally obvious: as much as Jerusalem is now in Rome, the Jewish city within the pagan capital, so the woman behind Peter may symbolize the church established out of Judaism, and the woman behind Paul the church established out of the Gentiles. The slightly later church of Santa Sabina on the Aventine would confirm the possibility of such an allegorical interpretation: there, on the west wall, a long mosaic shows two women, one described as *Ecclesia ex circumcisione* (the church from circumcision), the other as *Ecclesia ex gentibus* (the church from the Gentiles).

The magnificent mosaic in Santa Pudenziana portrays Christ seated on the throne in the centre, holding an open book in his left hand. *Dominus conservator ecclesiae Pudentianae* the text says—The Lord is the protector [or preserver] of the Pudentian church. His right hand is raised in the manner of a public speaker, and the apostles are shown in positions of earnest debate. Paul, too, holds a book in his hand, but the text shown here is no longer the original one.

The importance of this mosaic is further highlighted by one word in the book held by Christ: *Conservator*, instead of the usual Latin Christian *salvator*. In Latin inscriptions, *conservator*, meaning protector or preserver, was a title given to emperors and to the highest pagan godhead, Jupiter. So the people who used it here, instead of the normal Christian term *salvator*, were implying that Christ had taken over: he was the man on the throne, the one who displaced both the 'divine' emperors and the highest of the pagan gods. The world, Jerusalem and Rome, East and West, were now under Christ's rule. Suetonius' vague account, when he wrote about the tumult 'instigated by Chrestus' in Rome under Claudius, had become more true than ever. Christ was present, and he ruled over all.

The American scholar Fredric W. Schlatter recently pointed out that this inscription could have been added to the mosaic just after AD410, when the Goths under Alaric sacked Rome. The Goths, Christians themselves, intended to spare the churches, but marauding soldiers destroyed or damaged some of them nonetheless. Santa Pudenziana was spared. Secular Rome was looted, and the pagan citizens accused the Christians of having caused the downfall of Rome. In fact, Augustine was inspired to write his *City of God* because of these accusations. If this is the context of the inscription, then the whole mosaic attains an even more profound meaning. It turns the tables, it demonstrates that Christ alone is the protector, the one and only *conservator*. And the noble cloaks worn by the Christ and the apostles in the mosaic can be interpreted in terms of a real takeover: Christ clad as an emperor on his throne, the apostles as senators in the Rome senate.

The mosaic in Santa Pudenziana, therefore, symbolizes and sums up what early Christian tradition, from the first house-churches to official state recognition and the assumption of power, was able to achieve in Rome. Peter, Paul and, above all and above them all, Christ enthroned. Jerusalem and Rome not as opposites or contenders, but as partners, as integral and complementary parts of the whole.

This is one of the great examples in Christian history where the original Jewish Christian and the Gentile Christian roots of the church are put on an equal footing. In reality, Jewish Christians and their theology had long been pushed aside, actively neglected, consciously suppressed. But in Rome, at a time when Christians had the financial and political power to build their first real churches, the well-preserved memory of their origins had to be documented. At a place like Santa Pudenziana, where both Peter and Paul were remembered as guests, more so than anywhere else.

It is, however, important to note that the church did not employ such displays of victorious grandeur everywhere in the Empire. In Britain, the Christian house at Hinton St Mary, Dorset, is fourth century. It had a mosaic pavement portraying the Christ and the Christian Chi-Rho symbol (taken from the Greek alphabet, the first two letters of Christ's name). The frieze from the house at Lullingstone, Kent, which depicts *orantes*, people in positions of prayer, is also fourth century. Both can now be seen at the British

Museum. Simple fourth- and even fifth-century house-churches have been found at Augsburg and Mühlbach in south-east Germany.

The youthful, beardless Christ of Hinton St Mary, a beautiful work of art in its own right, hints at the very human side of Christian belief. Here, Christ is not the imperial protector, he is the young, accessible companion of men and women, portrayed in the manner often also found in very early statues of the 'good shepherd'. And he is tangible—not high up in an apse, but down on the floor. The Christians of Hinton St Mary had not forgotten that Christ, the Lord, was also the downtrodden, lowly, crucified Son of Man. Perhaps the wealthy owners of this preciously decorated villa knew that the worldly triumph of Christianity was as dangerous to the purity of the faith as it was outwardly beneficial to the greater glory of God.

10
The Spreading Flame

Wherever the first Christians may have met together in Rome, whether in the houses of those mentioned in Paul's letters or elsewhere, and whether they permanently set aside special rooms for their services or not, the evidence points to a number of quite large private homes. And we should not necessarily think of these first Christian house-churches as consisting of a handful of people only. Even when, in Ephesus, after the departure of Aquila and Priscilla, Paul could not find a suitable private house and had to rent a meeting place, he did not go for small premises, but rather for the 'lecture hall of Tyrannus' (Acts 19:9). This building probably belonged to a teacher of that name (a name frequently found on inscriptions at Ephesus) who let it when he did not need it, similar to the way the premises of colleges are let during the long vacation. One such lecture hall is known to have existed next to the library of Celsus at Ephesus.

Lecture hall, tentmaker's house, senator's villa, high-rise flat—there was certainly no lack of places to meet. Only the catacombs must be excluded for New Testament times— Christian use of these burial grounds cannot be demonstrated before the second century.

Peter's task

It is not difficult to envisage scenes in which Peter is preaching and talking about his experiences with Jesus before and after the crucifixion. And it is not difficult either to compare such a scene with the one depicted in a second-century relief found at Ostia, the harbour of Rome. Here, a man is lecturing from a kind of platform, with people listening and debating in the background, and to the left and right two scribes are taking shorthand notes on wax tablets, each consisting of six wooden frames. In just the same way as Matthew-Levi may have taken shorthand notes of Jesus' speeches, so people at Rome (where the technique had been refined after all, long before Peter's time) could have made arrangements for a couple of stenographers to write down Peter's words.

When Peter finally left Rome, and the Roman Christians asked his companion and colleague Mark to compose a literary account of Peter's lectures, Mark would have had a handy collection of notes at his disposal for reference. Remember the early church historian Papias and his statement that Mark was Peter's *hermeneutist*, his interpreter in the figurative sense (as we saw in chapter 3). Using those shorthand wax tablets for the content, Mark would have structured the material, giving it its literary form and order. Peter, as we know, eventually ratified the final version and had it sent to recipients abroad. Copies were sent to Jerusalem and beyond, to Qumran.

We find a hint of Peter's despatch of gospel scrolls from Rome in a New Testament letter. The second letter of Peter has traditionally (and by a slowly growing number of modern scholars) been ascribed to Peter himself. Even critics of Peter's authorship tend to identify the place of origin of the letter as Rome. If Peter himself did write it, it *could* be dated to the last year or years of his life: the text reveals that he is fully aware of his impending death. Our earliest sources maintain that he died in the aftermath of the persecution under Nero or, more precisely, in the fourteenth year of the emperor's reign (which lasted from 14 October AD54 to his suicide on 9 June AD68). 'I think it is right to refresh your memory as long as I live in the tent of this body,' Peter writes, 'because I know that I will soon put it aside, as our Lord Jesus Christ has made clear to me. And I will make every effort to see that after my departure you will always be able to remember these things.' (2 Peter 1:13–15)

It is a veiled statement. 'Departure' here of course means death—one of the rare examples where the context shows that death is actually meant, not the literal act of going away. The 'soon' of verse 14 should be translated as 'suddenly'. This, in any case, is what the Greek word used here usually means. And it would fit a man who was probably in his late sixties by the time he came to Rome for the second time in around AD59 (assuming that he and Jesus were of approximately the same age)—a decidedly old man in those days.

If this estimate is correct and if Peter is in fact the author of this letter, then a date *before* the fire of Rome and Nero's persecution of AD64/65 is equally plausible, for the letter does not mention anything relating to the devastating fire and the persecution. On the contrary, in places where one might even expect them, in those famous apocalyptic verses of chapter three, they are conspicuously absent. Neither a 'forger' writing later under Peter's name, nor Peter himself writing in Rome after the great fire and the ensuing persecution is likely to have avoided making at least a passing allusion to these events in such a letter. I tend to think that the letter should be dated, for reasons of language, style and content alone (leaving authorship aside) to around AD62 at the latest. But this is not the time or place to argue this controversial point.

What interests us here is what is written in verse 15 of the first chapter: 'I will make every effort to see that... you will always remember these things.' What is the 'effort' he intends to make? It cannot refer to the letter itself, as some scholars have thought. This letter, concentrating as it does on a few selected aspects of Peter's teaching, cannot represent the whole number of 'these things' alluded to earlier in verses 10, 12 and 15. Here, the full gospel is meant, the gospel of the 'eternal kingdom of our Lord and Saviour Jesus Christ' (2

Peter 1:11). Therefore, some commentators (perhaps as early as Irenaeus in the second century, although this is uncertain) have regarded this passage as a reference to Mark's Gospel—the one Gospel, after all, written under Peter's direct influence.

Indeed, some unmistakable references to Mark can be seen in 2 Peter. 2 Peter 1:8, with its talk of 'fruitfulness', echoes Mark 4:19, a saying of Jesus. The account of the event on the Mount of Transfiguration in 2 Peter 1:16–18 is an interesting eyewitness variation ('we are eyewitnesses') of Mark's account in Mark 9:2–13—also based on Peter. So important was this event that Peter takes it up again in his second letter—compare this to the way in which Paul tells the story of his conversion on three different occasions! 2 Peter 3:17 refers to an admonition by Jesus in Mark 13:5 that his followers should not be deceived and led astray, and there are many more such connections and 'echoes', not least with the speech of Jesus on the Mount of Olives in Mark 13:3–37.

The 'effort' Peter refers to, then, is probably his undertaking to have as many copies as possible of Mark's Gospel sent to the recipients of his letter. And these, according to 2 Peter 3:1, are identical with those listed at the beginning of his first letter: Jewish and Gentile Christians in Pontus, Galatia, Cappadocia, Asia and Bithynia. In other words, five scrolls at least were needed, and considerably more if possible.

An interesting aspect of this 'background story' is provided by the oldest surviving papyrus codex of 2 Peter, the p72, written in the third century. Here, the Greek word for 'making an effort' is not in the future, but in the present tense. If this reading, which is corroborated by one of the two oldest parchment codices, the Codex Sinaiticus, and by one other, later manuscript, should prove to be correct—then we would have Peter saying that he is already in the process of doing it: 'I am making every effort'. And this would further underline the historical situation in the early sixties of the first century. Peter tells his readers that the process has already been set in motion. Copies of Mark's Gospel have been in circulation for some time, but there are very few scribes available to the Christian community in Rome, and it does take some time to write a whole gospel on a papyrus scroll. Now, however, it is down to you, in Pontus, Galatia, and so on: 'I am making every effort'.

And there is one last shred of evidence—precarious perhaps. Amongst the tiniest of papyrus scraps found in cave Seven at Qumran, there is one with just six visible letters on two lines. The papyrologist José O'Callaghan suggested that this fragment, 7Q10, if it is from the New Testament, could be 2 Peter 1:15. It is much too small to be identified with any degree of certainty, but what O'Callaghan did not even think of when he suggested 2 Peter 1:15 is the circumstantial plausibility of his proposition. Since there was one copy (at least) of Mark's Gospel in cave Seven at Qumran, a copy of 2 Peter alongside it would have made sense. After all, it would be regarded as the 'apostolic authentication' of the Gospel...

Greek or Latin?

Peter and Mark wrote in Greek although they were writing from Rome. But wasn't Latin the 'official' language of Rome, the language of the Empire? And what about the Latin inscription put on the cross by Pontius Pilate and recorded in John's Gospel: 'It read, Jesus of Nazareth, the king of the Jews. Many of the Jews read this sign, for the place where Jesus was crucified was near the city, and the sign was written in Aramaic, Latin and Greek.' That Roman soldier who left a fragment of Virgil's *Aeneid* at Masada in around AD73, does he not underline the fact that Latin was a language imported to Palestine? Did Jesus himself speak not only Greek, but also Latin? For example, what language did he speak when he met the Roman centurion at Capernaum and the Roman procurator in Jerusalem?

The situation is complex. In New Testament times, and in the preceding and following decades, Latin was, of course, the language of Roman literature. It was also the official language of administration (hence its appearance on the cross). The philosopher Seneca wrote Latin as cultured and sometimes as contrived as possible, and the satirist Petronius wrote in Latin, purposefully imitating the vulgar language of the masses but demonstrating his mastery of elevated style as well. Persius, Juvenal, Tacitus, Suetonius, Pliny the Elder and Pliny the Younger and many others—they all wrote in Latin, and whenever we find references or allusions to Jews and Christians in their works, they are of course in Latin. The proper language of first-century Rome was Latin, not Greek. And it was the language of the great poets.

On the other hand, Rome was changing in the first century. Juvenal, in his third satire, complains: 'I no longer like the city as a Greek one... for some time, the Syrian Orontes has flowed into the Tiber and has brought with it the language and customs and, with the flute, the sloping chords of the harp, and tambourines which are at home in the east, and girls who offer themselves for sale at the circus.'

Syria and the Orontes—which rises in Lebanon and flows north through Syria into Turkey, where it turns west to the Mediterranean—are used here to represent the whole of the east of the Empire where Greek was the common language, regardless of other native tongues. Obviously, the melting-pot of Rome had incorporated so many people from the Greek-speaking East that they had turned Rome 'Greek', much to Juvenal's displeasure.

The same sort of picture is painted by Seneca, in AD42, the year of Peter's first journey to Rome. In his essay to his mother Helvia *On Consolation*, he writes: 'Look at these masses of people for whom even the roofs of enormous Rome are hardly sufficient: the largest part of this crowd is without a fatherland. They have swarmed together from their towns and colonies, even from the whole world... Have them all summoned by name and ask them, "Where is your home from whence you came?" and you will see that the greater part have left their ancestral domiciles and come to this city, which is certainly the greatest and most beautiful, but not their own.'

Again, most of these people would not have brought Latin with them, but the lingua franca of the Empire, Greek. This includes the Jews, of course, who had come and were still coming from the East. As a matter of fact, Jews from outside Palestine, from Antioch or Alexandria, for example, had adopted Greek to such an extent that they needed Greek translations of the Old Testament. One of the reasons behind the translation of the Old Testament into Greek in the third century BC, was precisely this growing inability to understand written Hebrew, let alone spoken Aramaic. It has even been doubted, by sceptics, whether Philo of Alexandria, the greatest Jewish scholar of New Testament times, knew Hebrew at all. Flavius Josephus, the Jewish historian who was a slightly later contemporary of the New Testament authors, wrote his book in Greek, struggling at first: he himself admitted that his Greek was clumsy initially, but he persevered, because he wanted to be understood by as many people as possible, not least at the court in Rome. He did not bother to learn Latin: Greek came first. And even most of the inscriptions found in the Jewish catacombs of Rome are in Greek, with only a very few in Latin.

The 'masses' from the East used Greek as their common language—a crude, unrefined, everyday Greek. On the other hand, the literary and philosophical elite in Rome knew Greek and tended to show off with it, since it was the language of the great Greek poets and philosophers. Titus, the emperor who lived from AD39 to 81, is said by his biographer Suetonius to have known both Latin and Greek so well that he could make speeches and write poems in both languages and improvise as he went along. Tiberius, however, who lived from 42BC to AD37 and was the emperor under whom Jesus was crucified, knew Greek well but avoided it in public, as Suetonius tells us. He once prohibited a soldier, who had been asked, in Greek, to testify, from answering in any language but Latin. Claudius, the emperor of the Jewish-Christian expulsion from Rome in AD49, knew Latin and Greek well enough to invent three new letters, on the basis of Greek ones, and to add them to the Latin alphabet. He spoke Greek with Greek legates and wrote historical books in Greek.

So the 'educated classes' were bilingual, no matter which language they preferred. And the middle and lower classes spoke Latin if they were born Romans, and Greek (plus their native tongues) if they were immigrants or descendants of immigrants from the East. The latter group made up the majority of the first Christian missionary 'target groups'. Indeed, Greek would have been preferred by Christian writers, since the better educated people, even Roman ones, would have understood it anyway. (Although they would probably have smiled at the rough-hewn style and vocabulary.)

Jesus and his followers may have picked up some Latin from the Roman soldiers whom they would have met on their travels in Palestine. But they would not have seen any reason to perfect their knowledge of it. When Paul wrote to the Romans, he wrote in Greek as a matter of course; when Mark and Peter wrote in and from Rome, they did not hesitate to use the common language of their readers—Greek.

On the other hand, Roman Christians with Latin language connections would have existed in New Testament times. There are traces of them in the names we find in Paul's letter to the Romans: Urbanus, Priscilla, Aquila, Rufus, Junias, Ampliatus, Julia. The names alone do not imply that these people were born in Rome (Aquila, as we know, came from Pontus). But it does show that Latin names and therefore elements of Latin were not alien to Jews and Jewish Christians.

Some adapted to the Latin used in their environment. It has been shown many times that Mark's Gospel is full of Latinisms. The most obvious example is found in Mark 12:42, where he explains that two copper coins make one 'quadrans'—a coin which was not in circulation in the east of the Empire. In Mark 15:16, it is explained that the (Greek) palace is a (Latin) *praetorium*. A very few scholars have even suggested that Mark's Gospel was originally written in Latin; but this would run counter to the attitude of the first Christian authors whose strategy it was, in obedience to Jesus' command, to reach the world with his message. Mark, however, does take into account those readers and listeners whose Greek was so inadequate that they needed at least the Latin equivalents for technical terms.

The church—the body of Christian believers—hesitated for a long time before using Latin as an 'official' language. The first literary Christian documents in Latin were the *Octavius* of Minucius Felix, around AD 166, and the writings of Tertullian, Cyprian and Novatian. At this time, the first Latin translations of (parts of) the New Testament would have appeared as a matter of course. The time was ripe. The *Acts of the Scillitan Martyrs*, discussed in a previous chapter, were written in Latin, in AD 180. The scrolls in the *capsa* mentioned in these *Acts* may have been in Greek, but they may equally have already been in Latin by that time. The letter of Paul and the Gospels, with Acts, appear to have existed in Latin by AD 180.

But this is long after the period covered by this book. The choice of Greek in preference to Latin as the language of mission to the Empire was well thought through, given the circumstances—a brilliant implementation of Jesus' call to take the gospel to the ends of the earth. Latin later took over, with Jerome's Latin Vulgate Bible in the early fifth century. Times had changed and Latin was to remain the world language for the next thousand years. It was this Latin version which shaped our own western culture. But it would never have come into existence had it not been for the original texts, in the common language of the first centuries. These had prepared the ground and reached the ordinary people in the street as well as the philosophical, cultural and political elite.

'Quo vadis?'

When all is said and done, Jesus appears once more in Rome. Or so that tale in the *Acts of Peter* tells us. This is the *Quo vadis?* story, which gave Henryk Sienkiewicz the title for the novel for which he was awarded the 1905 Nobel prize for literature, and which made Peter Ustinov a world star when he played Nero in the movie of 1951.

As is the case with the rest of the *Acts of Peter*, well-established facts and novelistic inventiveness are difficult to disentangle. According to the story here, told in around AD180, Peter is persecuted by men whose wives and concubines were refusing to sleep with them, having heard Peter preach on chastity. They threaten him with execution. His friends persuade him to flee: they want him to go on serving Jesus. Hesitantly, he complies. But as soon as he leaves the city gates, he sees Jesus approaching. 'Lord, where are you going?' he asks him. (In Latin, this is *Domine, quo vadis?*) Jesus replies: 'I am coming to Rome to be crucified.' Peter asks: 'Lord, are you being crucified again?' And Jesus replies: 'Yes, Peter, I am being crucified again.'

Peter understands. He sees Jesus ascend into heaven, returns to Rome and explains his decision to stay and face crucifixion. The prefect Agrippa and his soldiers take Peter prisoner. Agrippa accuses him of 'atheism'—that welcome false charge used by the representatives of Roman state religion against Christians—and sentences him to death by crucifixion. Peter, who desires a lowlier form of execution than that of his Lord, asks to be crucified head downwards. His executioners do him the favour, mockingly perhaps, and are not over-taxed by it: this form of crucifixion, with the head towards the ground, was well-known and listed among the gorier forms of punishment and torture in Seneca's essay *To Marcia, On Consolation*, written around AD41.

After Peter's death, the previously uninformed Nero accuses the prefect Agrippa of having spoiled his own show. He, the emperor, had intended to punish Peter much

163

more cruelly and severely since Peter had converted some of his servants to Christianity. But Nero is told in a vision to stop persecuting and destroying Christian communities. He obeys, and no more Christians are persecuted by him after the death of Peter. All this is told in the *Acts of Peter*.

Visitors to Rome can still see the chapel of *Domine quo vadis* on the Via Appia, just outside the Porta Capena. Those keen on tangible objects of veneration can even see the impression of Jesus' feet preserved in the ground—similar to the one in the little Ascension Chapel on the Mount of Olives in Jerusalem (has anyone ever dared to compare sizes?). One can almost see the Jerusalem and Roman Christians rushing to the spots with wet plaster... They did a good job too, at the site of the church of Santa Francesca alla Romana: here, the imprint of Peter's knees is preserved, traces of his fervent prayer before a contest with his enemy, Simon the Magician (also mentioned in the *Acts of Peter*). With such truly impressive evidence, one almost does not dare to look for the serious background to these entertaining and edifying stories (and it is quite obvious that this is exactly what they were meant to be).

There is, however, a more gracious way of coping with such stories. I experienced it once when I visited the abbey of Tre Fontane in Rome. Here, at the Three Fountains, Paul was very probably executed. It is the old Roman *Aquae Salviae* where condemned Roman citizens died by the sword. The story goes that Paul's head, having been cut off, touched the ground three times before coming to rest, and that on each spot a fountain sprang forth. Chapels were built—their successors are still there today—and a place of pilgrimage was inaugurated. People came to collect the water for medicinal purposes, expecting miracle healings, but the whole thing proved to be somewhat counter-productive when, in later centuries, the water turned out to be malaria-infested.

Only in the last century have Trappist monks from La Trappe in France installed themselves at Tre Fontane, sanitized the area and established a community in the thirteenth-century Cistercian abbey. Ever since, it has been one of the rare, beautifully quiet places in Rome where a spirit of tranquillity and meditation is in the air among the eucalyptus trees. When I spoke to the monk dealing with visitors (the only Trappist allowed to speak), he looked at one of the fountains and said about the story of Paul's head: 'The church smiles upon such legends.'

But even in the *Acts of Peter*, the skeleton facts are there: the crucifixion of Peter in Rome, documented by other, independent sources, even that it was head downwards; the death of Peter unrelated to the fire of Rome and the following persecution, but before the death of Nero; the punishable offence of atheism; members of the imperial court as Christians, and many other examples throughout the novel, some of which we looked at in previous chapters.

But what about Jesus' appearance to Peter on the Via Appia? The novel does not demand that this incident be taken seriously as hard fact (neither does it demand this of Peter's final address on the cross). The apparition of Jesus, set here at the end of the apostolic, the strictly-speaking New Testament, period in Rome, serves a different purpose.

In Peter's death Christians are seen to experience the second great separation of their young history. After the death of the earthly Jesus in Jerusalem, now the 'rock of the church' is going to die. Human self-interest protests: he must not go, we need him, others need him—let him flee until the danger is past. After all, he had done so once already, escaping from prison and probably from death, in Jerusalem (Acts 12:9–17). Why not again? This time his task has been fulfilled. Mark's Gospel and two letters are written, the teaching is secure, all sectors of society had been reached with the word of Christ. And so it is Peter's turn to 'stretch out his hands' on the cross, as Jesus had prophesied to him (John 21:18–19).

As in many examples of later world literature to the present day, including the distortions of novels such as Nikos

Kazantzaki's *Last Temptation of Christ*, Jesus is used in literature, outside the New Testament, for recognizable purposes. Not all of them are evil by definition.

This last, concluding and conclusive apparition of Jesus at the gates of Rome reminding Peter to take up his cross, still has a message for all those who are securely grounded in the historical facts, who are not irritated by the imaginative interpretations of fiction—indeed, using our imaginations can sometimes help us to see things afresh. The following words from Mark's Gospel were known to readers of the *Acts of Peter* as they are known to us:

'Then Jesus called the crowd to him along with his disciples and said: "If anyone would come after me, he must deny himself and take up his cross and follow me. For whoever wants to save his life, will lose it, but whoever loses his life for me and for the gospel will save it. What good is it for a man to gain the whole world, yet forfeit his soul? Or what can a man give in exchange for his soul? If anyone is ashamed of me and my words in this adulterous and sinful generation, the Son of Man will be ashamed of him when he comes in his Father's glory with the holy angels."' The *Acts of Peter* wants to make its readers face this message—and it is still facing us today.

We have come full circle in our quest for the roots of our knowledge about the historical Jesus. And yet it is comforting to know that new discoveries will be made tomorrow, new insights gained, new connections realized. W. B. Yeats' play *The Resurrection*, written in 1931, sums up the challenge both to the inquisitive and to the patiently faithful mind. It is a dialogue between a Greek and a Syrian.

The Greek Why are you laughing?

The Syrian What is human knowledge?

The Greek The knowledge that keeps the road from here to Persia free from robbers, that has built the beautiful human cities, that has made the modern world, that stands between us and the barbarian.

The Syrian But what if there is something it cannot explain, something more important than anything else?

The Greek You talk as if you wanted the barbarian back.

The Syrian What if there is always something that lies outside knowledge, outside order? What if at the moment when knowledge and order seem complete, that something appears?

How do we know about Jesus? We have very clear instructions: test everything and hold on to the good (1 Thessalonians 5:21); examine the Scriptures every day to see if it is true (Acts 17:11); accept that many things have remained untold, since the whole world would not have room for the books that would need to be written (John 21:25). We must also measure the results of research, be they secure or hypothetical, against the yardstick of those eyewitnesses who 'did not follow cleverly invented stories' (2 Peter 1:16); of those whose testimony is true (John 19:35); and of those who affirm, by their own authority, that it is true (John 21:24) and based on careful investigation from the beginning (Luke 1:3).

In a letter dated 13 June 1878, the poet Gerard Manley Hopkins wrote to the clergyman Richard Watson Dixon: 'The only just judge, the only just literary critic is Christ, who prizes, is proud of, and admires, more than any man, more than the receiver himself can, the gifts of his own making.' There is humility, trust, and creative optimism in these lines. Three virtues which might serve us well—not only for all the searching and close questioning which is the never-ending task of the scholar, but also for the 'testing' to which we are all committed. So that, even looking at the limited array of sources and information surveyed in this book, we may come to know, like Theophilus in the dedication to Luke's Gospel, 'the certainty of the things we have been taught'.

Bibliography
and books for further reading

This bibliography is not comprehensive. It contains easily available publications which may help to broaden the subject matter of this book. Books or articles explicitly or implicitly referred to in the preceding pages are marked with an asterisk; although some of these are suitable for general reading, others are of a rather technical nature and some are not in English. However, for further reading, only English language publications have been chosen.

P. Ariès/G. Duby (eds.), *A History of Private Life, Vol. 1: From Pagan Rome to Byzantium*, Cambridge, Mass./London, Harvard University Press, 1987.

*L. W. Barnard, 'The "Cross of Herculaneum" Reconsidered', in: W. C. Weinrich (ed.), *The New Testament Age. Essays in Honor of Bo Reicke*, Vol. 1, Macon, Georgia, Mercer University Press, 1984.

*A. Barnes, *Christianity at Rome in the Apostolic Age*, London, Methuen, 1938.

*R. A. Batey, 'Jesus in the Theatre', *New Testament Studies*, 30, 1984.

R. Bauckham/R. T. France/M. Maggay/J. Stamoolis/C. P. Thiede (Consulting eds.), *Jesus 2000. A major investigation into history's most intriguing figure*, Oxford, Lion Publishing, 1989.

*G. G. Bilezikian, *The Liberated Gospel: A Comparison of the Gospel of Mark and Greek Tragedy*, Grand Rapids, Baker, 1977.

C. Blomberg, *The Historical Reliability of the Gospels*, Leicester, IVP, 1987.

F. F. Bruce, *New Testament History*, London, Oliphants, 1977.

F. F. Bruce, *Men and Movements in the Primitive Church*, Exeter, The Paternoster Press, 1979.

F. F. Bruce, *Jesus and Christian Origins outside the New Testament*, London, Hodder, 1984.

J. Carcopino, *Daily Life in Ancient Rome. The People and the City at the Height of the Empire*, Harmondsworth, Penguin, 1956, repr. 1986.

*C. M. Carpano *et al.*, *Roma Sotteranea e Segreta*, Milan, Arnoldo Mondadori, 1985.

H. Chadwick, *The Early Church*, Harmondsworth, Penguin, 1986.

*V. Corbo, *The House of St. Peter at Capharnaum*, Jerusalem, Franciscan Printing Press, 1972.

J. M. Cotton/J. Geiger (eds.), *Masada: The Latin and Greek Documents*, Jerusalem, Israel Exploration Society, 1989.

J. Drane, *Jesus and the Four Gospels*, Oxford, Lion Publishing, 1984.

J. Drane, *The Bible: Fact or Fantasy?*, Oxford, Lion Publishing, 1989.

J. D. G. Dunn, *The Evidence for Jesus*, London, SCM Press, 1986.

*G. Edmundson, *The Church in Rome in the First Century*, London, Longmans, Green & Co., 1913.

*J. K. Elliott, 'Codex Sinaiticus and the Simonides Affair', *Analecta Vlatadon* 33, Thessaloniki, The Patriarchal Institute for Patristic Studies, 1982.

*A. Fackelmann, 'Präsentation christlicher Urtexte aus den ersten Jahrhunderten, geschrieben auf Papyrus. Vermutlich Notizschriften des Evangelisten Markus?', *Anagennesis*, 1, 1986.

*G. D. Fee, *I and 2 Timothy, Titus*, San Francisco, Harper and Row, 1984.

E. Ferguson, *Backgrounds of Early Christianity*, Grand Rapids, Eerdmans, 1987.

R. L. Fox, *Pagans and Christians—In the Mediterranean World from the Second Century AD to the Conversion of Constantine*, London, Penguin, 1986.

R. T. France, *Matthew*, Leicester, IVP, 1985.

R. T. France, *The Evidence for Jesus*, London, Hodder, 1986.

R. T. France, *Matthew—Evangelist and Teacher*, Exeter, The Paternoster Press, 1989.

169

S. Freyne, *Galilee, Jesus and the Gospels*, Dublin, Gill and Macmillan, 1988.

*J. Fugmann, *Römisches Theater in der Provinz. Eine Einführung in das Theaterwesen im Imperium Romanum*, Stuttgart, Gesellschaft für Vor–und Frühgeschichte in Württemberg und Hohenzollern, 1988.

M. Green, *Evangelism in the Early Church*, Crowborough, Highland Books, 1990.

*R. H. Gundry, *Matthew. A Commentary on his Literary and Theological Art*, Grand Rapids, Eerdmans, 1982.

D. Guthrie, *New Testament Introduction*, Leicester, IVP, 1990.

*A. von Harnack, *The Mission and Expansion of Christianity in the First Three Centuries*, 2 vols., New York, Harper, 1962.

M. Hengel, *Studies in the Gospel of Mark*, London, SCM Press, 1985.

*G. Kennedy, 'Classical and Christian Source Criticism', in: W. O. Walker (ed.), *The Relationships among the Gospels*, San Antonio, Trinity University Press, 1978.

*Y. K. Kim, 'Palaeographical Dating of p46 to the Later First Century', *Biblica*, 69, 1988.

*J. Kürzinger, *Papias von Hierapolis und die Evangelien des Neuen Testaments*, Regensburg, Friedrich Pustet, 1983.

*K. Lake, *The Earlier Epistles of St. Paul, their Motive and Origin*, London, Rivingtons, 1914.

*H. Lehmann, 'Wolfgang Helbig (1839–1915)', *Mitteilungen des Deutschen Archäologischen Instituts, Römische Abteilung*, 96, Mainz, Philipp von Zabern, 1989.

*S. Loffreda, *Recovering Capharnaum*, Jerusalem, Franciscan Printing Press, 1985.

*P. Maas, *Textual Criticism*, Oxford, Oxford University Press, 1958.

I. H. Marshall, *I Believe in the Historical Jesus*, London, Hodder, 1977.

C. Mason/P. Alexander, *Picture Archive of the Bible*, Oxford, Lion Publishing, 1987.

P. Merkley, 'The Gospels as Historical Testimony', *The Evangelical Quarterly*, 58/4, 1986.

A. Millard, *Discoveries from the Time of Jesus*, Oxford, Lion Publishing, 1990.

*J. O'Callaghan, 'New Testament Papyri in Qumran Cave 7?', *Journal of Biblical Literature,* Supplement, 91, 1972.

*J. O'Callaghan, 'The Identifications of 7Q', *Aegyptus,* 56, 1976.

*B. Orchard/H. Riley, *The Order of the Synoptics,* Macon, Georgia, Mercer University Press, 1987.

*B. Pixner, 'An Essene Quarter on Mount Zion?', *Studia Hierosolymitana, I: Studi Archeologici,* Jerusalem, 1976.

*B. Pixner, 'Wege Jesu um den See Gennesaret', *Das Heilige Land,* 119/2–3, 1987.

*M. Prior, *Paul the Letter-Writer and the Second Letter to Timothy,* Sheffield, Sheffield Academic Press, 1989.

*R. Riesner, 'Essener und Urkirche in Jerusalem', *Bibel und Kirche,* 40/2, 1985.

*R. Riesner, *Jesus als Lehrer,* Tübingen, J. C. B. Mohr (Paul Siebeck) 1988.

*C. H. Roberts/T. C. Skeat, *The Birth of the Codex,* Oxford, Oxford University Press, 1983.

*J. A. T. Robinson, *Redating the New Testament,* London, SCM Press, 1976.

J. A. T. Robinson, *The Priority of John,* London, SCM Press, 1985.

*F. W. Schlatter, 'The Text of the Mosaic of Santa Pudenziana', *Vigiliae Christianae,* 43, 1989.

*B. Schwank, 'Das Theater von Sepphoris und die Jugendjahre Jesu', *Lebendiges Zeugnis* 32, 1977.

*B. Schwank, 'Ein griechisches Jesuslogion?', in: N. Brox et al. (eds.), *Anfänge der Theologie. Festschrift J. B. Bauer,* Graz-Wien-Köln, Styria, 1987.

*B. Schwank, 'Die neuen Ausgrabungen in Sepphoris', *Bibel und Kirche,* 42, 1987.

*C. Simonides, *Facsimiles of Certain Portions of the Gospel of St. Matthew, etc.,* London, Trübner & Co., 1861.

J. H. Skilton (ed.), *The Gospels Today. A Guide to Some Recent Developments,* Philadelphia, Pennsylvania, Skilton House Publishers, 1990.

*M. Smith, *The Secret Gospel,* Wellingborough, The Aquarian Press, 1985.

*B. Standaert, *L'Évangile selon Marc: Composition et genre littéraire,* Brugge, Sint-Andriesabdij, 1978.

G. N. Stanton, *The Gospels and Jesus,* Oxford, Oxford University

Press, 1989.

H. Staudinger, *The Trustworthiness of the Gospels*, Edinburgh, Handsel Press, 1981.

W. H. Stephens, *The New Testament World in Pictures*, Cambridge, Lutterworth Press, 1989.

J. Stevenson, *A New Eusebius*, Rev. ed. by W. H. C. Frend, London, SPCK, 1987.

*K. E. Stevenson/G. R. Habermas, *The Shroud and the Controversy*, Nashville, Thomas Nelson, 1990.

G. Theissen, *The Shadow of the Galilean*, London, SCM Press, 1987.

*C. P. Thiede, *Simon Peter—From Galilee to Rome*, Exeter, The Paternoster Press, 1985; Grand Rapids, Zondervan, 1988.

*C. P. Thiede, 'A Pagan Reader of 2 Peter. Cosmic Conflagration in 2 Peter 3 and the "Octavius" of Minucius Felix', *Journal for the Study of the New Testament*, 26, 1986.

*C. P. Thiede, 'Babylon, der andere Ort: Anmerkungen zu 1 Petr 5,13 und Apg 12,17', in: C. P. Thiede (ed.), *Das Petrusbild in der neueren Forschung*, Wuppertal, R. Brockhaus Verlag, 1987.

*C. P. Thiede, 'Rom, neutestamentliche Zeit (Archäologie)', *Das Grosse Bibellexikon*, Vol. 3, Wuppertal/Zürich, R. Brockhaus Verlag, 1989.

*C. P. Thiede, *The Earliest Gospel Manuscript? 7Q5 and its Significance for New Testament Studies*, Exeter, The Paternoster Press, 1990.

*C. P. Thiede, 'Papyrus Bodmer L. Das neutestamentliche Papyrusfragment p73 = Mt 25,43/26,2–3', *Museum Helveticum*, 47/1, 1990.

H. W. Tajra, *The Trial of St. Paul. A Juridical Exegesis of the Second Half of the Acts of the Apostles*, Tübingen, J. C. B. Mohr (Paul Siebeck), 1989.

*V. Tzaferis, 'New Archaeological Evidence on Ancient Capernaum', *Biblical Archaeologist*, 46, 1983. (And other, unpublished, material.)

G. Vermes/M. D. Goodman, *The Essenes According to the Classical Sources*, Sheffield, Sheffield Academic Press, 1989.

*D. B. Wallace, 'The Majority Text: A New Collating Base?', *New Testament Studies*, 35, 1989.

D. B. Wallace, 'John 5,2 and the Date of the Fourth Gospel', *Biblica*, 71/2, 1990.

More titles from LION PUBLISHING

THE BIBLE: FACT OR FANTASY?

John Drane

Miracles, people rising from the dead, a man who claimed to be God—the Bible contains some sensational material. If these things really happened, they are vitally important for all time.

But is the Bible 'true'? Has its truth been disproved by discoveries in history, archaeology or science? Do the Bible's stories and its teaching still ring true today?

John Drane, Lecturer in Religious Studies at Stirling University, Scotland, has written popular introductions to the Old and New Testaments, and the best-selling *Jesus and the Four Gospels*. He has presented religious programmes on television. His doctoral research was on the Gnostics. In this book he brings his talents as a scholar and communicator to bear on the central question of the Bible's trustworthiness and relevance today.

ISBN 0 7459 1300 8

CHRISTIANITY ON TRIAL

Colin Chapman

This book sets out the case for and against Christian beliefs in a way that invites a verdict.

Colin Chapman has put together a collection of over 1,000 quotations, representing the greatest thought from the first century to the twentieth. They cover the deepest human questions. Christian claims are set out, tested and compared with alternatives from other major religions, thinkers and ideologies.

ISBN 0 7459 1273 7

THE WAY OF JESUS

Dr Bruce Farnham

Many today are curious about the life of Jesus. What is the truth about the stories of his life, his teaching, his death—and rising again? How can we understand them today?

This book is written for the many who simply want to find out about the life and teaching of Jesus, founder of Christianity. The author has lived for many years in the Middle East, and has experienced at first hand both the misunderstandings about Jesus and people's curiosity about who he really was.

Dr Bruce Farnham is a scientist by training. He has written for others who, like himself, are living and working in a world which is both increasingly secular and also torn by religious ideologies. It is vital that people from many backgrounds, especially those from other religions, understand the facts and fallacies about the life of Jesus, and how his message is understood today.

ISBN 0 85648 880 1

A selection of top titles from LION PUBLISHING

THE BIBLE: FACT OR FANTASY? John Drane	£2.99 ☐
CHRISTIANITY ON TRIAL Colin Chapman	£5.95 ☐
WHOSE PROMISED LAND? Colin Chapman	£4.99 ☐
THE WAY OF JESUS Bruce Farnham	£2.25 ☐
FOR THE LOVE OF SANG Rachel Anderson	£3.99 ☐
LOVE NEVER ENDS Jenny Richards	£2.99 ☐
DOUBT Os Guiness	£4.95 ☐
SPIRITUAL AWAKENING Shirwood Eliot Wirt	£4.95 ☐
SPIRITUAL POWER Shirwood Eliot Wirt	£5.99 ☐
PILGRIMS' LONDON Robert H. Baylis	£4.99 ☐

All Lion paperbacks are available from your local bookshop or newsagent, or can be ordered direct from the address below. Just tick the titles you want and fill in the form.

Name (Block letters) _____

Address_____

_____

Write to Lion Publishing, Cash Sales Department, PO Box 11, Falmouth, Cornwall TR10 9EN, England.

Please enclose a cheque or postal order to the value of the cover price plus:

UK: 80p for the first book, 20p for each additional book ordered to a maximum charge of £2.00.

OVERSEAS INCLUDING EIRE: £1.50 for the first book, £1.00 for the second book and 30p for each additional book.

BFPO: 80p for the first book, 20p for each additional book.

Lion Publishing reserves the right to show on covers and charge new retail prices which may differ from those previously advertised in the text or elsewhere, and to increase postal rates in accordance with the Post Office.